SIKH WOMEN IN ENGLAND
their religious and cultural beliefs and social practices

SIKH WOMEN IN ENGLAND
their religious and cultural beliefs
and social practices

Satwant Kaur Rait

Trentham Books
Stoke on Trent, UK and Sterling, USA
and the
COMMUNITY RELIGIONS PROJECT
Department of Theology and Religious Studies
University of Leeds

Trentham Books Limited

Westview House   22883 Quicksilver Drive
734 London Road   Sterling
Oakhill   VA 20166-2012
Stoke on Trent   USA
Staffordshire
England ST4 5NP

© 2005 Satwant Kaur Rait

First published 2005

British Library Cataloguing-in-Publication Data
A catalogue record for this book is available from the British Library

ISBN-13: 978-1-85856-353-4
ISBN-10: 1-85856-353-4

Designed and typeset by Trentham Print Design Ltd, Chester and printed in Great Britain by Alden Press Ltd., Oxford.

Contents

About the author • vii

Foreword • ix

Acknowledgements • xi

Introduction • xiii

Research methods used in the study • xix

Chapter 1
A Background to the life of Sikh women • 1

Chapter 2
Religious values • 17

Chapter 3
Women in Sikhism and Sikh Society • 47

Chapter 4
The Social Life of Sikh women • 55

Chapter 5
Cultural values • 95

Chapter 6
Listen to me • 127

Chapter 7
Conclusion • 159

Bibliography • 169

Glossary • 173

Index • 185

*Dedicated
to
Sikh women,
who live for others
not for themselves*

About the author

Dr Satwant Kaur Rait was born in the village of Lambra in the Hoshiarpur district of the Punjab (India), following the tradition of having the first child at the maternal grandparents' home. At the age of five, she was admitted to a local school where she passed the Higher Secondary Examination and won a scholarship to go to university. Instead, however, she took a course in Librarianship and got a government job, which enabled her to graduate and do an MA in Delhi. She worked in that job until she got married. She had an arranged marriage and migrated to Leeds to join her husband in 1968.

She studied in Leeds so that she could get a professional job in a library and her determination, strong willpower and support from her husband helped her in acquiring a professional qualification in Librarianship. She got her first job in 1974. Between 1974 and 1986 she led a very busy life combining family, career and research. Although she started at the bottom, by 1986 she had become a Principal Officer and was also appointed as a Justice of the Peace on the Bradford Bench. She received her PhD from Loughborough University in 1993, by which time she had many books, reports and research articles to her name.

She has two children who have always remained her first priority in spite of her many other commitments. They are appreciative of their loving and caring upbringing. As a family, all are very close and supportive of each other. Dr Rait has kept her religious and cultural values very close to her heart. Her deep attachment to Sikh culture and the plight of some Sikh women in India and England has inspired her to write on this theme. This book contains the women's perception of the social, cultural and religious traditions of Sikhism and reflect the collective experience of many Sikh women. Among Dr Rait's publications, those specifically related to the Punjabi culture are: *Dictionary of Punjabi Name Elements* (1984), *Acquisition and Cataloguing of Punjabi Language Literature in British Public Libraries* (1985) and *Punjabi Rasoi Kala* (1989).

Foreword

The Community Religions Project was initiated in 1976 in the Department of Theology and Religious Studies at the University of Leeds in order to encourage research on religions in the West Yorkshire area. In the years that followed it extended its interest to religions in other parts of Britain, its primary focus remaining the manifestation of religious communities within particular localities or regions. Research has been undertaken by staff members, doctoral students, and those working on relevant undergraduate and postgraduate dissertations. Research funds have been obtained from a number of grant-awarding bodies. Since the Project's inception it has published research papers and, from 1986, a series of monographs.

This book, on Sikh women in England, is based on research conducted in the Leeds area. It was researched and written by an independent scholar, Dr Satwant Rait, in association with the Community Religions Project. In interviews with women of all ages, Dr Rait has investigated social, religious and other cultural issues, relating these to Punjabi traditions and the British context. Her work is informative for policy makers, scholars, Sikhs themselves, and all those interested in knowing more about a group of women who have made an important contribution to the local economy, community and culture. It is instructive on the issues that concern Sikh women and on their hopes and expectations.

Dr Rait worked in the library service before her retirement. She is now an active researcher pursuing further studies on Asian women and on the history of Sikh *gurdwaras* in Britain. She is committed to hearing and presenting the personal histories of local Sikhs.

Kim Knott
Community Religions Project
August 2004

Acknowledgments

I have always been keen to write about Sikh women because of my personal experience and knowledge of their collective experience. In 1999, I was awarded a grant by the Scarman Trust to write a report on Sikh women in Leeds through the Indian Women's Association. I am grateful to Alison Haskins, the Regional Director of the Trust in Yorkshire, for supporting me whole-heartedly and being so understanding of the subject area. The survey I conducted for that report gave me an insight into the practical difficulties of gathering personal information and also made me determined to complete the work and disseminate the findings. After completion of the report, limited copies were printed and circulated for comments, including one to John Battle M.P. He took an interest in the work and encouraged me to produce an 'easy to read' version which was published in 2003. Funding was received from Awards For All, for printing and launch costs. For all these efforts my source of support was Alison Haskins and my thanks go to her. I am also indebted to Dr. Kim Knott of the Department of Theology and Religious Studies at the University of Leeds, who originally encouraged me to develop the research into an academic monograph to be published by her department. The monograph was prepared but the success of the version for the general reader and the feedback we received encouraged us to think of making some changes in the format. It was decided that I would give most of the source material for reference and further research at the end of every chapter in order to retain the natural flow, though on occasions there are references in the text. Some changes have also been made to the original manuscript and the present document attempts to cover Sikh religious, social and cultural traditions and values as they have developed in England.

It is not possible for one person alone to accomplish a study like this, and the original project was a group effort, run through the Indian Women's Association. The data was collected through fieldwork in Leeds and I would like to thank the women who provided invaluable help and information for the study. Unfortunately, all those deserving recognition cannot be named individually as their identities must not be disclosed for reasons of confidentiality. I hope that those women whom I interviewed and spoke to during the survey will accept a general expression of gratitude. I would also like to thank them for spending their valuable time in answering my numerous queries in the group discussions. The women I interviewed were honest and sincere when responding to my questions, giving me a real insight into their lives and the manner in which the Sikh community generally regards issues affecting women. They were patient, understanding and cooperative.

I must emphasise, however, that although the views and opinions in this study came from the women, the analyses and expression are my own. I alone take responsibility for any errors and inadequacies. I hope that I have avoided any embarrassment to any person by my guarded treatment of quotations and references. I would also like to state that this is by no means just an academic exercise. My approach was to make this an informative and readable document based on the real-life experience of contemporary Sikh women. I attempted to portray women of different ages, backgrounds and experiences in a sympathetic and objective way, therefore writing with both my head and heart. I tried to be fair and unbiased. Direct communication and cross-examination gave me an insight and understanding of what the women were relating.

It is customary to give credit to one's own family and friends, and in this case it is heartfelt. My husband Harbhajan Singh, has been an enormous source of strength and inspiration and he has encouraged me to persevere despite the difficulties I have with partial sight. I am lucky to have a family that is supportive of one another's work and I must thank my children Greta and Jas who willingly read and commented on this script. Two friends of mine, Tanya and Susan, also deserve a note of appreciation for reading the final version of this book.

Introduction

This study concentrates on Sikh women in England – their religious, social and cultural values and experiences and how these have changed over the years. The information on which it is based was collected from March 2000 to June 2001, though a few interviews were conducted in 2004 to update the study. I consciously decided to concentrate on Sikh women rather than all Asian women in order to study their particular values and traditions in depth and with understanding. I also wanted to produce a report of use to agencies keen to understand the specific needs of Sikh women, which are not always similar to those of other Asian women. To complete the spectrum of the lives of Sikh women, I decided to include women from Sikh-related sects, which represent a different interpretation of some Sikh traditions and values. I have also analysed and compared the values of first generation migrants with those of British-born Sikh women.

My own wide-ranging experience of life as a woman struggling to establish my own identity, becoming a person in my own right, and the experience of living in a traditional Punjabi culture in Britain helped me to make this study thorough and objective. I am a Sikh woman born in the Punjab to a traditional but educated family. After Partition, my family moved to Delhi where I was brought up and educated. I received a university education, which was uncommon amongst Sikh women at the time. I worked in India before migrating to Leeds after an arranged marriage. I became aware that I had to acquire some additional qualifications if I wanted to get a professional job in the UK. After gaining such qualifications I got my first job in Leeds and then worked in three other local authorities (Kirklees, Bradford and Derbyshire), progressing to senior positions. I carried out research alongside my family and career responsibilities, which resulted in many publications. My own background and the experience of working with Asian communities in this country has given me an insight into Sikh traditional values; my linguistic skills have eased the communication with non-English-speaking Sikh women in interviews and helped me to grasp subtleties of meaning. My work experience in India and England has made it easy for me to converse with women of varied backgrounds, and my community-oriented work has given me the techniques and skills to abstract and analyse information objectively.

There is a lack of original material written on the operative cultural, religious and social values of the Sikh community. Studies of this nature, written from the viewpoint of a sociologist, are few and far between. One can trace some scattered material written on different aspects of this subject such as *Marriage Practices of Sikhs* by Surinder Kaur Jyoti (1983), which covers the changing trends in spouse selection among Sikhs, and Wazir Singh's *Sikhism* and *Punjab's Heritage* (1990), a collection of edited essays on Punjab's culture and Punjabi heritage. Sharan-jeet Shan's *In My Own Name* (her autobiography written in 1985) is the story of a Sikh who had an independent mind and tried to assert her own autonomy. It deals with the status of women, arranged marriages and the operation of the dual-value system in the Sikh community. Amrit Wilson's *Finding a Voice: Asian Women in Britain* (1978) reflects the views of Asian women on love and arranged marriages and the changes occurring within Asian communities in Britain. It also relates their experiences of racism in daily life and at work, housing, education, law and immigration policies.

These books and the works of two British scholars, Roger Ballard and Catherine Ballard, proved invaluable for this research. Some of the essays and articles produced by the two Ballards, individually and jointly, on migration, traditional cultural values, changing life style and the growing generation gap among Sikhs were based on the outcome of intensive fieldwork. The essays on 'Conflict, Continuity and Change: Second Generation South Asians' by Catherine Ballard (1979) and 'Changing Life Style among British Asians' by Roger Ballard (1986) offer examples of a growing generation gap affecting British-born Sikhs, including women. The articles in *New Community* on 'Family Organization among the Sikhs in Britain' by Roger Ballard (1972) and on 'Arranged Marriages in the British context' by Catherine Ballard (1978) are of direct relevance to this research. Parminder Bhachu's *Twice Migrants* is an anthropological study, which presents useful information on East African Sikhs and their preservation of traditional values. Some locally-based pieces of research relevant to this topic are Beatrice Drury's 'Sikh Girls and the Maintenance of an Ethnic Culture' (1991) conducted in Nottingham, Beryl Dhanjal's impression of 'Sikh Women in Southall' (1976), Raminder Singh's *The Sikh Community in Bradford* (1978), S. S. Kalra's *Daughters of Tradition* (1980), S. S. Kalsi's *The Evolution of a Sikh Community in Britain*, T. Thomas and P. Ghuman's *A Survey of Social and Religious Attitudes among Sikhs in Cardiff* (1976).

There are a number of books available on the Sikh religion. For the purposes of this research, my main sources were the Sikh scripture *Guru Granth Sahib* and *Sikh Rahit Maryada* (Sikh Code of Conduct). I also consulted Harjot Oberoi's *The Construction of Religious Boundaries* (1994). This book details the culture, identity and diversity in Sikh traditions. Surinder Singh Johar in his *Handbook on Sikhism* (1977) endeavours to explain in simple language the basic tenets of Sikhism, its growth and the factors that contributed to its development. Avtar Singh's *Ethics of the Sikhs* (1991) has attempted to produce a systematic and scientific study of Sikh ethics based on the entire Sikh corpus, from the *Guru Granth* to the codes and manuals which followed the creation of the *Khalsa* by *Guru* Gobind Singh. Along similar lines, Surinder Singh Kohli's *Sikh Ethics* is a short treatise based on the *Adi Granth*. McLeod's book on *Sikhism* (1990) is a useful explanation of textual sources for the study of Sikhism. This list would not be complete without Khushwant Singh's *The Sikhs* (1953), Harbans Singh's *The Heritage of Sikhs* (1985) and Teja Singh and Ganda Singh's *A Short History of the Sikhs* (1989).

Not only are Sikhs one of the noticeable communities even in India, with their unique characteristics, but they are also one of the most visible Indian immigrant communities in a number of other countries. In Canada, James G. Chadney wrote about *The Sikhs of Vancouver* (1984). He covered not only immigration patterns and the economic arena but also Sikh traditions and beliefs in a foreign land. This is a general and useful book though it lacks a woman's perspective.

The study on Sikh women from a sociologist's point of view led me to view my own contribution as seeking to provide both background information on Sikh women and an examination of their normative and operational values. This information was gathered from Sikh women through interviews held in an informal setting and through group discussions in consultation meetings. Following this method, I tried to portray not only traditional views but also the views of British-born Sikh women. Indeed, Sikh women born and brought up in this country experience a number of forces which run counter to orthodox and traditional values, thus creating a new Sikh identity. A number of sensitive issues arose during the interviews (not unexpectedly) suggesting difference, change and compromise.

Sikh women are defined as those who accept Sikh teachings, not necessarily those baptised or born into Sikh families. The pattern of growth of Sikh communities is reproduced throughout England. Although the major part of my research was conducted in Leeds it is applicable further afield as it is the case that the experience of Sikh women all over the country has been broadly similar. The Sikh community country-wide is small and has settled mainly in the industrial towns of England such as Birmingham, Bradford, Derby, Leeds, Leicester and London. Many of the women in Leeds have moved here from other parts of the country for reasons of marriage or employment. There are close contacts between the various urban communities and attendance at family functions gives them ample opportunity to discuss changes affecting family life.

Punjabi terms are used in the text, as the use of such terminology is natural and gives authenticity to a document so closely associated with the community. They are transcribed, but not formally transliterated because of the difficulty of adding diacritical marks on the computer keyboard. Punjabi words are given in italics and their meanings in English within brackets. A glossary of Punjabi terms is provided at the end of the text.

Following an account of the methods used for this study, the first chapter of the book deals with the background of Sikh women, their migration and settlement patterns, their identity and Sikh cultural norms and values. The second chapter examines Sikh religious values and the third chapter is about the women in Sikhism and Sikh society. The fourth chapter concentrates on the social life of Sikh women, and the fifth on their cultural values, discussing marriage, dowry, the joint family system and the folk traditions. The sixth chapter is a collection of the life stories of a few Sikh women and chapter seven is the conclusion.

Research methods used in the study

The primary aim of this study is to provide an insight into the cultural, religious and social lives of Sikh women in this country. This research illustrates not only the traditional values inherited from the Punjab, but also the gradual absorption of British values. This reflects an enormous capacity on the part of Sikh women to restructure and reshape their own values, enabling them to adjust within an alien culture. Sikhs have become an integral part of multicultural Britain. Interaction between the communities exposes them to one another's traditions and values and it is important, therefore, that the fundamentals of Sikh traditions are understood by the younger generation of British-born Sikhs as well as by the host community. With better understanding it is possible to avoid the biases and stereotypes often projected by the British media on issues such as arranged marriage, dowry and joint families. I hope this study will contribute towards a more sophisticated appreciation of the rich and dynamic Sikh culture.

The information for this study was collected through unstructured interviews. Firstly, informal, conversational interviews were held with women on a one-to-one basis. This approach ensured the women did not feel inhibited. Secondly, I arranged consultation meetings to encourage group discussion. The interviews were conducted in Punjabi and English using general prompts and questions. Punjabi was used mainly with older and middle-aged East African Sikh women and women who originated from the Punjab. English was used with British-born Sikh women. Women were interviewed at their convenience and at a venue suitable to them – mainly in their homes – in a relaxed environment. They were encouraged to talk freely about whatever they liked. It was important to listen to their perspective if they deemed it relevant in order to obtain a comprehensive view. Interviewing them in their own homes provided me with an added opportunity to observe interactions within families. I learnt about the differences between individuals and generations, and about the engagement between Indian and British culture and traditions. In order to avoid distraction, I did not take notes at the time of the interview, but recorded the information immediately afterwards.

A guide questionnaire was prepared in order to maintain consistency between the interviews. It included open-ended questions about personal details, background and the women's experience in Leeds and in other places where they had lived before. I initially contacted the women, introduced myself to them, then explained the purpose of the research and finally asked if they were willing to participate. Appointments were made with those subjects who were prepared to take part.

The sample consisted of one hundred and fifty women, made up of approximately fifty direct migrants from India, fifty who had migrated from Africa and fifty younger women who migrated for marriage either from India or Africa or were born and brought up in this country. The selection of this sample was made by using various sources, that is to say contacts offered by other women and contacts given by community organisations, women's groups and any other group where women meet, such as religious places or day centres. The sample included young, middle-aged and elderly participants.

The women were generally open and honest about their situations, with a few exceptions where women covered up certain situations affecting their family honour and prestige. It should be acknowledged that it is not always easy to share one's family and personal secrets with an outsider. On the whole, I was heartened by their responses and felt trusted and valued.

In the group discussions only general topics were raised and sensitive issues were avoided in order to save women from any embarrassment. I held many workshops at venues where women were accustomed to meet. Elderly women's groups met regularly in two Sikh *gurdwaras*, and in one centre operated by the Social Services Department. There were also ladies' *satsangs* held in most *gurdwaras* in Leeds, which involved middle-aged and elderly women. Three groups were found that met in the houses of individual women on a regular basis. All these groups were widely consulted on specific topics such as popular beliefs, dowry and so on. In order to gain a wider view, a consultation day was also held at a neutral venue in order to give access to all women irrespective of their allegiance to different *gurdwaras*. Workshops were held at the West Yorkshire Playhouse on prominent issues affecting Sikh women. Sikh women of all ages were consulted collectively through the discussions and workshops on different topics. The women were not merely interested but also enthusiastic about sharing their views. This consultation increased their trust in me and also empowered them with confidence and openness. In addition to the women interviewed, another one hundred women were consulted in this way.

I also used other practical methods often utilised in the social sciences, such as participation and observation. Without this, the data collected by other methods could not have been interpreted objectively. I used this approach with Sikh-related groups such as the *Namdharis, Radhasoamis* and *Nirankaris*. I visited their *gurdwaras* and places of meeting frequently and tried to participate in as many events as possible. I attended their functions and ceremonies, such as anniversaries, weddings, birthdays and *namkaran* (name giving), in order to observe the similarities with, and differences from, mainstream Sikhism. As 'an observer-as-participant', I was observing and learning by participation, but known by all to be studying the group. I was asking questions and interpreting the data collected, but not taking part in a more active sense.

These visits to Sikh temples allowed me to establish contact with more women. As I wanted to gather further information on values and traditions, it was necessary to observe and question those involved. This was done through 'total participation': becoming an inconspicuous member of the group. I participated in community festivals, attended cultural, social and religious functions in Sikh *gurdwaras* and other venues in order to gather such information. I spent almost all the weekends of my research period in *gurdwaras*, which are the main centres of religious and social activities for Sikhs. I talked to women whilst totally involving myself in all activities. This brought me into direct contact with young women and girls, enabling me to listen to their views. It also gave me the opportunity to listen to the comments, criticisms and community gossip, which helped me, in some cases, to judge the adequacy of my account. I also had discussions with women I met in functions in towns other than Leeds just to find out the consistency of operative values within the Sikh community living in England.

A survey of this nature often creates difficulties for the researcher. It was time-consuming to interview so many women in such a short time as they wanted to talk about many issues and problems irrelevant to this study. Most women were helpful and prompt, but some forgot the pre-arranged dates or told me on my arrival that they were busy. Some had to be contacted more than once, and after many contacts would eventually say 'No'. A few women promised to come to my house for reasons of confidentiality and neither came nor rang. I found my way around these problems by being assertive and proactive and by telephoning them before leaving my home. I had difficulties when interviewing younger women, as I first had to make contact with their mothers, some of whom would not allow their daughters to be interviewed. Many of those who did liked to sit through the interview, so the young women had to give me socially acceptable answers and not those in their hearts. Where pos-

Women's consultation

sible, I tried to contact young women through the institutions they attended or to strike up casual conversations in the *gurdwara*.

I found that there was a poor response to written publicity and not a single reply was received to letters and posters sent to training centres. Similarly there was hardly any response to the posters displayed in Leeds Metropolitan University and the colleges of higher education where there are a number of Sikh students. Finally, I decided to contact young women directly and explain the purpose of my study. Some came forward, but others were afraid to share their experiences. Most women were frank in their responses, but a few were wary where issues involving family prestige were concerned. The Sikh community is relatively small and information gets passed around in the same way as family sagas do. However, this sometimes worked in my favour by allowing me to hear all sides of a story.

I was often annoyed and affected by the limited roles of women and the expectations placed on them in the Sikh community, as well by the failure of some men to credit me with the seriousness I thought my study deserved. There were also other attitudes and responses, which occasionally impinged on the process of data collection. For example, some Sikh women would not participate in or come to a venue associated with a particular caste or sect. Some *gurdwaras* were helpful, whereas others did not show any interest. This was a challenging study for me, as a Sikh woman, to conduct. In the process, I tried to avoid bias and to maintain the promised confidentiality.

1

A background to the life of Sikh women

Britain has always been a home for migrants from all over the world. It has a rich diversity of different faiths and cultures. A significant minority of its population originates from the Indian sub-continent and Sikhs form a part of the Indian community. The background of Sikh women in this country will be portrayed through a discussion of their numbers, settlement patterns, the identity of individuals who make up this population and an examination of their allegiance to, and identification with, cultural and religious sub-groups. It is also important to discuss the cultural norms and values on which the behaviour of Sikh women is based.

Sikh origins

Sikhs mainly originate from the Punjab, a state in northern India, where they form the majority of the population, although the Sikh community comprises only 2% of India's total population. Sikhs have a strong sense of being a separate community, based on a distinct religion (Sikhism), a regional culture and the language of the Punjab (Punjabi).

Prior to the partition of India in 1947, the original geographical area of the Punjab contained a wide range of people including Sikhs, Hindus and Muslims, all of whom were encompassed in one generic term 'Punjabi'. Punjab, which means *punj* (five) *ab* (water) was a land of five rivers: Jhelum, Chenab, Ravi, Beas and Sutlej. It lies in the North West of the Indian sub-continent and is now divided between India and Pakistan. Partition divided the Punjab on the basis of religion; East Punjab became part of the Indian territory and home to Sikhs and Hindus, while West Punjab formed part of Pakistan and provided a home to Muslims. East Punjab was further divided in 1966 into three units. Punjab

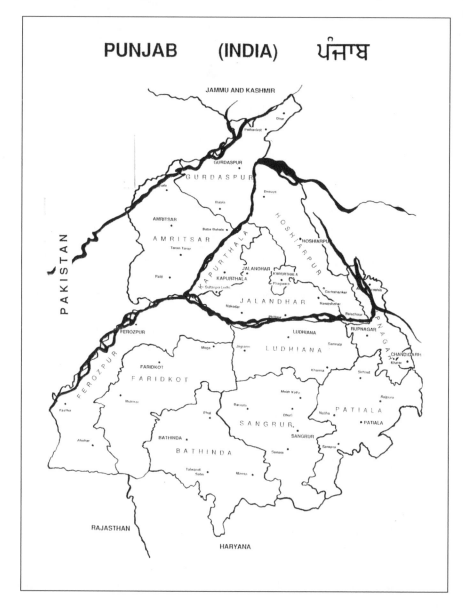

became the Punjabi-speaking area, Haryana being the Hindi-speaking region and Chandigarh the capital. Punjab and Haryana are now separate, while Chandigarh remains a Union Territory and the capital of both Punjab and Haryana. Sikhs are primarily Punjabi, for they claim Punjab as their homeland. Punjabis of any religion and region speak the common language called Punjabi, though it is written in three different scripts: Arabic, Devanagri and Gurmukhi. Sikhs use the Gurmukhi script.

The present Punjab is a fertile region divided by the Beas and Sutlej rivers. Between the rivers lies the rich, fertile area of Doaba (land between two tributaries). It comprises the districts of Jullundhur, Kapurthala, and Hoshiarpur. Two small towns, Jandiala and Nakodar, are in the south of Jullundhur. South of the river Sutlej lies Malwa, and the largest town in this area is Ludhiana. To the east of Ludhiana is the modern state of Chandigarh; to the west is Ferozpur and to the South is Patiala, Nabha and Jind. Between the Beas and Ravi rivers lies Majha, which contains the holiest place of Sikhs, the city of Amritsar.

Size of the Sikh community

It is difficult to assess accurately the number of Sikh women in England. The 2001 Census identified people by religion for the first time. It collected information about ethnicity and religious identity and Sikhs appeared as a separate entity. According to the Census the number of Sikhs living in England is 327,343 which represents 29% of the Indians living in this country. However, this number is approximate and inaccurate as the response to this question was optional. The Census has given further categories of males and females and the number of Sikh women is quoted as 163,716.

There are also local sources of statistics such as religious bodies and Community Relation Councils. The estimates provided by religious groups are based on their own membership and the religious adherence to that group. Statistics produced by such bodies have limited reliability. It is important to bear in mind that there may well be differences between an expression of size in terms of 'the community', the membership of the place of worship and the number of its regular religious adherents. *Gurdwaras* produce membership lists and the Sikhs listed on them are mainly male, even though membership is open equally to male and female Sikhs. Very few females become members. It is not compulsory for all members of a religious group to become members of their religious institutions, so such lists are not comprehensive and do not truly reflect the status of the whole Sikh community. Community Relations Councils also keep statistics on the basis of religion, but none provides accurate statistical information on the number of Sikhs living in this country.

Settlement patterns

The whereabouts of relatives, friends and compatriots of pioneer migrants from the same linguistic and cultural group often influence the early settlement pattern of any non-indigenous community. The availability and affordability of housing also dictate where people settle. Settlement patterns tend to change when a community becomes more established. Initial Sikh settlement in this country was in industrial areas such as London, Birmingham, Coventry, Derby, Leeds, Bradford and other cities where work was readily available.

Sikhs initially bought large run-down properties. One of the early female migrants in this study reported that her family bought their first house in the early 1950s. Subsequently, other relatives and friends bought houses nearby. The reasons she gave for buying this property were that it was spacious, cheap and it was convenient to travel to work and into town.

The concentration of Sikhs in any area was the most influential factor in establishing the Sikh *gurdwara*. The places of worship provided by, and for, the Sikh community used to correspond largely to this settlement pattern. This was true in the earlier stages of settlement, but is not applicable now. As the Sikh community became more settled and established, they started moving into more affluent and suburban areas and buying better and expensive properties. They do not have to depend on public transport since most families own a car and thus it is no longer necessary to live near *gurdwaras*. The number of *gurdwaras* also grew with the expansion of the Sikh community in this country. With the arrival of East African Sikhs, *gurdwaras* began to be opened on the basis of caste. Indian communities in East Africa were used to having social and cultural institutions based on caste loyalties; as East African Sikhs came to this country and found themselves in the majority, they wanted to set up their own caste-based *gurdwaras*. Some of the East African Sikhs were the disciples of *Baba* Puran Singh, a highly revered Sikh *sant* (saint) in East Africa, and his followers opened *gurdwaras* based on his teachings.

Sikh identity

Sikhs appear to be a homogenous and cohesive group, but closer examination reveals that the internal organisation varies somewhat. They do not always identify themselves as Sikhs, but prefer to associate with one another on the basis of other factors such as caste, region or sect.

It is important to consider Sikhs in broadly different categories, as there is a great deal of diversity in their lifestyles and beliefs. There are also cultural differences between rural and urban Sikhs, and Sikhs from East Africa. Generalisations about one social unit may not be applicable to another, despite the fact that most Sikhs originally hailed from India, and mainly from the Punjab.

This study indicates that most of the Sikh women living here originate from Doaba in the Punjab, mainly from the Hoshiarpur, Jullundhur and Kapurthala districts. Some came from Amritsar, Gurdaspur, Ludhiana and Ferozpur and the villages around these districts. Many Sikh women came from East Africa, and a few from Malaysia and Singapore. The East African Sikh women came from Uganda, Tanzania and Kenya, mainly from the cities of Nairobi, Nokoro, Darassalam and Mombassa. It is generally believed that Sikhs who migrated directly from India are traditionalists, with little experience of bureaucratic ways because of their rural background, as compared with East African Sikhs who display a knowledge of bureaucracy because of their urban experience (Bhachu, 1985). This may be true of males, but this survey found that there is a great deal in common between the attitudes and beliefs of Indian and East African Sikh women. Sikhs migrating from Singapore and Malaysia tend to be more prosperous, but do not display any distinctive characteristics, perhaps due to their small numbers.

Migration

Migration patterns have a direct bearing on behaviour, attitudes and lifestyles. Poverty is often assumed as a main reason for emigrating but this was not the only reason for Sikh families to leave their homeland, for the Indian state of the Punjab is currently the most prosperous and rapidly developing part of modern India. Rather, it was the Sikh tradition of migration that led many Sikhs to migrate. Their history shows them to be adventurous, hard-working and risk takers by nature. Another reason for emigration was the partition of India, which created social and economic problems. Those left destitute by Partition took advantage of the British economic boom and came to work in the industrial towns of this country.

The pressure of population growth on land and the scarcity of industrial employment were other factors. When the head of a family dies, his sons may divide up the land amongst themselves. If this means splitting up the holding into uneconomical units, one or more of the younger brothers may be asked to leave home to work elsewhere, with the other brothers contributing to the travelling costs. Experience has shown that money can be made in city jobs or abroad which, if invested in the family farm, can be used for improving the living standards of all the family, raising the productivity of the farm, paying for children's education or finding suitable husbands for sisters and daughters. It is important to realise that Sikh migrants who worked in England often continued to send money home to support their families in maintaining the essentially communal structure of the joint family.

A few Sikhs were already in England after World War II: ex-soldiers, students, professionals and businessmen. They helped other Sikhs to migrate. The main factors that lay behind Sikh migration at this point was post-war reconstruction and the subsequent expansion of the British economy. As the British economy began to boom after the War, unskilled labour was recruited from South Asia. Sikhs already living in England were instrumental in sponsoring the passage of other kinsmen over here to find work in British factories. Landless Sikhs migrated in the hope of a better life and greater opportunities.

East African Sikhs migrated originally from the Punjab to East Africa in response to labour opportunities. When the construction of the railways in East Africa began, a large number of Sikh craftsmen were recruited from the Punjab to work. Their migration to England was mainly for political rather than economic reasons, such as Africanisation and the policies of Idi Amin, although some came for further education and eventually settled here.

The specific reasons for the migration of Sikh women are altogether different. They came to join their husbands or their sons and families, or they came for marriage. Sikh women started arriving in the late 1940s. East African Sikhs came later in family units.

In summary, Sikhs migrated not because of grinding poverty but for other reasons, such as pressure on land, the effects of Partition, enhancing family status, advancing education, seeking better opportunities, and their adventurous nature and the long tradition of migration within the Sikh culture. Sikhs from East Africa came mainly for political reasons and this was a forced migration. The specific reasons for the migration of Sikh women as given in the survey are marriage in the case of young Sikh women, joining their husbands by married women, and to join sons and families by elderly women.

Sikh women have come from both rural and urban areas of Punjab, other states in India and from East Africa, Singapore and Malaysia bringing with them their own traditions and values. There are also growing numbers of British-born Sikh women. For the purpose of this study, Sikh women in this country are considered in four categories:

■ a) Direct migrants from rural areas of Punjab, mainly from the Doaba region. The majority of these are *Jats* (land-owning class), with a small minority of other castes such as *Ramgarhias* (village artisans), *Khatris* (mercantile group), *Bhatras* (palm-readers and *granthis*), *Chamars* (landless agricultural labourers and leather workers), *Jhirs* (water carriers), *Nais* (barbers) and other castes, such as *Julahas* (weavers).

b) Direct migrants from urban areas of India, mainly from cities like Delhi, Chandigarh, Ludhiana, Amritsar and Gurdaspur. They are educated and belong to many different castes.

c) East African migrants, mainly from the *Ramgarhia* caste, who arrived as a result of Africanisation in the late 1960s. A few Sikhs also came from Singapore and Malaysia.

d) British-born Sikh women.

It is my observation that urban Sikh women are generally better educated and more adaptable to new situations. They often consider themselves superior to Sikh women from rural areas, assuming that villagers are set in their ways and less well-educated. Similarly, villagers have their own beliefs and biases and are critical of urban behaviour and attitudes. East African women prefer to mix with East Africans, giving the impression that they feel they are superior.

Sikh women who migrated from India to East Africa had little or no education and were mainly housewives. They tried to learn and share skills relevant to running their domestic lives, such as cooking, embroidery and sewing. They formed close friendships and in this they were helped by the warm weather of East Africa which, like India, has a warm climate so women could easily go out and about. Additionally, women did not go out to work, with few exceptions, so could spend time with other women. In England, most Sikh women work and hardly have any spare time to socialise.

The caste identity
The caste system was strongly condemned by the Sikh *Gurus*. Despite this, it remains deeply ingrained in the Sikh community. Caste is a social structure based on one's occupation. It is determined by birth and there is no way that it can be changed. In the Punjab, it is also an economic relationship closely tied to the traditional village economy. In a village, the land-owning caste (*Jat*) controls the production and economy of the village. This caste pays for a share of crops grown on their land and for goods and services provided by artisans and other low-caste groups, through a mode of exchange called the *jajmani* system (patron-client relationship).

The Sikh community in this country belongs to the following castes:

■   *Jats*, land-owning agriculturists

- *Khatris*, merchants and mainly resident in urban areas
- *Ramgarhias*, an artisan caste of carpenters, blacksmiths and bricklayers
- *Nais*, barbers and messengers
- *Julahas*, weavers
- *Jhirs*, water-carriers
- *Bhatras*, astrologers and palm readers
- *Chmars*, landless agricultural labourers and leather workers

In the UK, Indian Sikh women from rural areas belong mainly to the *Jat* caste. In Punjab villages, *Jats* often dominate numerically, politically and economically. They are extremely proud of their heritage, thus carrying an aura of superiority about them. Other castes such as *Nai, Jhir, Julaha, Chamar*, and *Bhatra*, are considered by *Jats* as lower castes. *Khatris* are a business class and are numerically few; they consider themselves to be a higher caste than *Jats*. *Jats* consider *Ramgarhias* to be inferior to them, but East African *Ramgarhia* Sikhs do not view themselves as inferior. In East Africa, they became economically prosperous in the post-war period. They became successful entrepreneurs, middle and high-level administrators, and technicians. The community was also urbanised, being concentrated in a handful of towns. By the time some moved to Britain, they were already well versed in handling British institutions because they had migrated from one urban environment to another.

Sikh religion and religion-related groups
Sikh women are religious and religion dominates their lives. Sikhs have a unique external identity, which binds them together into the *Khalsa* brotherhood, but their internal divisions based on different sects and religious groups tell another story. In addition to mainstream Sikh religion, there are different religious groups and sects operating within the Sikh community, such as *Radhasoamis, Nirankaris, Namdharis*, and *Nishkam Sevak Jatha*. It is useful to summarise their beliefs and traditions as practised and interpreted by them.

The Sikh religion
Sikhs believe in God (*Akal Purakh*), in the ten *Gurus* (*Guru* Nanak to *Guru* Gobind Singh) and *Sri Guru Granth Sahib* (the

Holy Scripture of Sikhs). Sikhs should not believe in any other religious doctrine, and the *Guru Granth Sahib* is their guide. Sikhism is based on the ethics of *kirt karo* (work), *wand chako* (share what you earn with the less fortunate) and *naam japo* (recite the name of your Lord). Sikhism gives importance to the family, with family life being the medium of spiritual expression. The Sikh *Gurus* made *seva* (voluntary service) a prerequisite to spiritual development. They repeatedly emphasised that *haumen* (individualism or self-centredness) is at the root of the problems that an individual and society suffer. They stressed that one should free oneself of the five evil manifestations of *haumen* – lust, anger, greed, attachment and pride. It is also necessary to go through an initiation ceremony in order to become a *sampuran* (complete) Sikh.

Sikhism promotes gender and caste equality, human dignity and making an honest living. The practice of *langar* (the free kitchen) is important to Sikhism. This practice offers everyone, regardless of religion, caste or colour, a free meal in the *gurdwara*. After *ardas* (the concluding prayer), *prasad* (a sweet made of semolina, butter and sugar) is distributed followed by *langar*. Sikhs are also advised to carry out *sangat* (to sit in the company of good people), and it is one of the main reasons for attending the *gurdwaras*. This not only gives importance to the congregation but also a strong sense of fellowship and of belonging to the community. Sikhs are advised to abstain from intoxicants, adultery and polygamy. The Sikh *Rahit Maryada* (the Sikh code of conduct) gives general guidance to Sikhs for their daily life.

Radhasoamis

The term *Radhasoami* is made up of two words: *Radha* (wife or soul) and *Soami* (husband or Lord) which means the 'Lord of the soul'. According to *Radhasoami* beliefs, the *Satguru* (true teacher) is the giver of light. They believe in a *Guru* (teacher) in human form who will teach the meaning of *nam* (God's word) in order to attain spiritual unity with God. Their main emphasis is on the attainment of spiritual unity with God through *namsimran* (meditation on God's name). *Radhasoamis* do not believe in religious rituals. They sit on chairs and do not remove their shoes when praying.

The *Radhasoamis* display no pictures in the congregation hall, and place no religious books on a platform. Their *diwan* (religious meeting) culminates in a sermon, which is based on the *Sant* (saint) tradition of Northern India. *Prasad* is reserved for special occasions, such as the anniversary of the birth of their *Guru. Radhasoamis* use nuts in their *prasad,* served on plates and eaten with utensils rather than the fingers. *Radhasoamis* preach the importance of vegetarianism for achieving salvation. The tradition of *langar* (free kitchen) is also different in *Radhasoami* practice. *Radhasoamis* do not prepare *langar* every week, although at their headquarters in *Beas* in India, *langar* is prepared every day. It is given free to the poor, but other people buy it at a reduced rate.

Their *Guru* lives in Beas, which is a *dera* (headquarters) of *Radhasoamis* and has become their place of pilgrimage. The *Guru* nominates his successor when he feels that his end is near. The person chosen is usually his closest disciple. The *Radhasoamis* have a formal organisation in Britain. The National Secretary of the *Radhasoami satsang* is appointed by their *Satguru.* Local secretaries are responsible for looking after the affairs of local *satsangs* and they also are appointed by the *Satguru.*

Nirankaris
Baba Dyal (1783-1855) was the founder of the *Nirankari* movement in India. Later Buta Singh (1883-1944), a member of *Nirankari Darbar* raised a group called *Sant Nirankari.* The majority of *Nirankaris* living in England belong to this group and their beliefs and traditions differ from the *Nirankari* sect's. Buta Singh was succeeded by Avtar Singh. *Nirankaris* call their *Guru* Avtar Singh '*shahan shah*' (king of the kings). After his death, his son *Satguru* (true *Guru*) Gurbachan Singh became the leader of the *Nirankari* movement. In 1980, he was assassinated and his son Harder Singh took over the leadership. *Nirankaris* have their headquarters in Delhi where their *Guru* lives and it has become their place of pilgrimage. The *Nirankaris* publish literature in many languages for distribution to the public.

The *Nirankaris* strongly reject idolatry and ritualistic practices. They follow the teachings of their *Satguru* Avtar Singh and they hold *diwans.* Their *diwan* is called *sangat.* There is no ritual impurity among women at the time of childbirth or marriage, and ceremonies are fixed without consulting astrologers. No dowry is displayed at weddings and there are no payments for the perfor-mance of ceremonies. They reject the caste system and preach the oneness of God. They believe in the teachings of the Sikh *Gurus* but do not regard the *Granth Sahib* as their *Guru*, which makes them different from mainstream Sikhs. The *Nirankaris* nominate an elderly person to conduct their weekly *sangat*. This person sits on a platform and the congregation performs *matha-takna* (bow down), and leaves money on the platform. They sing *shabads* (hymns) from the *Granth Sahib* and *Avtar Bani* (com-positions of Avtar Singh). They do not recite *ardas* (concluding prayer) or distribute *prasad* at the end of their *diwan*. Usually they prepare *langar* (free food) for the congregation, which is served to men and women in the same hall. There is no particular initiation ceremony, but the *Nirankaris* whisper their secret *nam* (word) in the ear of new followers. The *Nirankaris* are allowed to eat meat and consume alcohol. They do not preach vegetarian-ism, but do not cook meat at their *bhawans* (*gurdwaras*).

Namdharis

This group's name originates from the importance their founder *Guru* Ram Singh placed upon the practice of *nam-japna* (recital or meditation on the name of God). In India, they are also known as *Kukas*, from the Punjabi noun *kuk*, which means 'shriek'. Many members of the cult attain states of ecstasy in their acts of worship, in which they dance and call out. The men are easily identified by the manner in which they tie their turbans (*sidhi* turban – *Namdhari* style).

According to *Namdhari* tradition, the tenth *Guru*, Gobind Singh did not die at Nander in 1708, but continued his mission under the name of Ajapal Singh. He installed Balak Singh as his suc-cessor, succeeded in turn by Ram Singh. He nominated his brother, Hari Singh, to lead the movement before his deportation to Burma. Before his death Hari Singh nominated his nephew, Pratap Singh, as leader of the movement. He in turn nominated his own son, the present *Namdhari Guru*, Jagatjit Singh, in 1959 to be the leader of the *Namdhari* Sikhs. This demonstrates their belief in the continuity of the tradition of the living *Guru*.

Namdhari Sikhs pay great respect to *Guru Granth Sahib* although they do not believe it to be their *Guru*. They make a distinction between the *Guru* and the *Granth Sahib.* Their living *Guru* takes precedence over the *Granth Sahib.* They believe in *namsimran* and the devotee must meditate in absolute silence. During *namsimran* sessions, the presence of *Guru Granth Sahib* is not obligatory. *Namsimran* is followed by *ardas,* which is different from the mainstream Sikh *ardas. Namdhari* Sikhs recite the names of their *Gurus* after the ten Sikh *Gurus.* The importance of living *Gurus* and their *ardas* distinguishes them from other mainstream Sikhs. The *Namdhari* initiation ceremony is called *nam-laina* (receiving the *Guru*'s word, or *gurmantar*). The *Gurumantar* is the secret bond between the *Guru* and his disciple, which must never be divulged. A *prasad* of dried fruit is usually distributed at the end of *Namdhari diwans.* They strongly believe in *daswandh,* which means donating one tenth of their earnings to their religion. *Namdhari* Sikhs are strict vegetarians. They eat food cooked by *Sodhis* (one who follows the code of the discipline of *Namdharis*) only and they are prohibited from consuming meat or liquor, smoking tobacco or visiting prostitutes.

Guru Nanak Nishkam Sevak Jatha

The leader of this *Jatha* (organisation) was *Baba* Puran Singh Karichowala, who migrated to East Africa in the 1930s where he began preaching the message of the Sikh *Gurus* and the importance of vegetarianism. He gathered many followers in East Africa. He came to Britain in the early 1970s and attracted a large number of followers in the Midlands, where they set up their first *gurdwara* in Birmingham, known as *Guru Nanak Nishkam Sevak Jatha. Babaji* died in June 1983.

Followers of *Baba* Puran Singh observe the Sikh code of conduct very strictly. They are *keshdharis* (those who do not cut their hair or beard) and initiated Sikhs. *Baba* Puran Singh's main emphasis was on *amrit chhako te singh sajo te nam japo* (take *amrit* and be proper Sikhs by keeping *rahit* and the Sikh symbols, and meditate on the name of God). They do not allow non-*amritdhari* (uninitiated) Sikhs to participate in the reading of the *Granth Sahib* at *Akhand-path* (continuous reading) and *Sadharan path* (ordinary religious reading) ceremonies. The *gurdwaras* established by his disciples do not have an elected management committee. The living *Babaji* (leader of the organisation) appoints the leader of the *Jatha* and they are accountable for their actions to *Babaji.* This accountability helps them to run these *gurdwaras* smoothly and effectively. Women are not allowed to take part in *Akhand path*. Other *santmat* traditions of this *jatha* distinguish them from mainstream Sikhism.

These Sikh-related religious groups highlight the religious diversity of the Sikh community. The importance of describing these groups lies in showing not only the diversity existing within Sikh community but also their different beliefs, values and traditions.

Cultural values

Culture is a collective way of life which develops gradually over centuries and is moulded by religion, history and other such influences and institutions. It is a collection of customs. In an ordinary sense, the word 'custom' is applied to a habitual practice, or a common way of acting. It thus encompasses not only those practices whose origins and justifications are derived from religious beliefs, but also those rooted in cultural traditions. Customs are not necessarily regulated or enforced by law. They are often long standing practices, fortified by religious beliefs or social traditions, which the community regards as morally binding.

Sikhs have some cultural values that are applied to judge personal behaviour and their status in the community. The most important of these are the concepts of *izzat, laaj* (honour), *sharam, haja* (modesty), *khidmat* (hospitality), *muhabbat* (cordial relations with family, friends, neighbours), *robh* (influence through wealth, high status or kind nature), *seva* (looking after elders, voluntary service for the community). They also value family unity and see this as a source of strength. These are the main cultural norms on which the behaviour of Sikhs is based and appraised. The changing lifestyle of Sikh women is having an effect on traditions, religious beliefs and cultural values, which will be illustrated in the following chapters.

Further Reading

Ahluwalia, M. M. *Kukas: The Freedom Fighters of Punjab*. New Delhi: Allied Publishers, 1965.

Ballard, R. and Ballard C. 'The Sikhs: the development of South Asian settlements in Britain'. In Watson, J.L. (ed.). *Between Two Cultures*. Oxford: Basil Blackwell, 1977.

Ballard, R. 'The Context and consequences of migration: Jullundhur and Mirpur compared'. In *New Community*, 11, 1983.

Census. Office for National Statistics. April 2001.

Ghai, D.P. *Portrait of a Minority: Asians in East Africa*. Nairobi: Oxford University Press, 1965.

Ghurya, G. S. *Caste and Race in India*. Bombay: Popular Prakashan, 1969.

James, A. G. *Sikh Children in Britain*. London: Oxford University Press, 1974.

Johnson, J. *The Path of the Masters*. Beas: Radha Soami Satsang, 1985.

Kalsi, S. S. *The Evolution of a Sikh Community in Britain*. Leeds: University of Leeds: Community Religion Project, 1993.

Kapur, D. L. *Call of the Great Master*. Beas: Radha Soami Satsang, 1972.

Nirankari, M. S. 'Nirankaris'. *Bulletin of Christian Institute of Sikh Studies*. 7 (1), 2-10, 1978.

Oberoi, H. *The Construction of Religious Boundaries: Culture, Identity and Diversity in the Sikh Traditions*. Delhi: Oxford University Press, 1994.

Peristiany, J. G. (ed.) *Honour and Shame: the Values of Mediterranean Society*. Chicago: The University of Chicago Press, 1966.

2

Religious Values

Sikhism

Sikhism plays a crucial role in the lives of Sikh women. In order to understand their values and behaviour, it is important to discuss the theory and main principles of Sikhism.

The word Sikh is derived from the Pali '*Sikkha*' or the Sanskrit '*Shishya*' meaning 'disciple'. The Sikhs are the disciples of their ten *Gurus*, or teachers, beginning with *Guru* Nanak (1469-1539) and ending with *Guru* Gobind Singh (d. 1708). The definition of a Sikh as given in the Sikh Code of conduct (*Sikh Rahit Maryada*, 1984:79) is that a Sikh is any person who believes in God (*Akal Purakh*), in the ten *Gurus* (*Guru* Nanak to *Guru* Gobind Singh), in the *Sri Guru Granth Sahib* (Holy Scripture of Sikhs), in the other writings of the ten *Gurus* and their teachings, in the *Khalsa* initiation ceremony (Baptism) instituted by the tenth *Guru*, and does not believe in any other religious system. The code of conduct also guides the Sikhs in their daily life, in the performance of religious duties, in the importance of the *gurdwara* (the Sikh place of worship), in reading the Holy book and living and working in accordance with the principles of *Gurmat* (guidelines given by the *Gurus*).

Guru Nanak, the founder of the Sikh religion, decided to crusade against fanaticism and intolerance, which had become the practice of the ruling class of Muslims, and against the meaningless ritual discrimination suffered by the lower castes and women which had become an integral part of Hindu life. The two prevalent religions, Hinduism and Islam, were being misinterpreted and misused by their interpreters. *Guru* Nanak, assessing the situation, wanted to find a path that would unite Hindus and Muslims and establish unity and equality in humankind. He also wanted a religion that would be practical and offer guidance for daily life, giving strength and self-recognition to the poor. Successive *Gurus* contributed towards the development and expansion of Sikhism. *Guru* Angad, the second *Guru*, developed the *Gurumukhi* script, which later formed the basis of the Punjabi language – a simple language easily understood by ordinary people – thus making knowledge accessible and available to everyone. At that time, knowledge and literacy were the prerogative of the powerful *Brahman* caste. *Guru* Angad also taught and wrote in Punjabi, instead of Sanskrit. By increasing the knowledge and independence of ordinary people, *Guru* Angad was able to undermine the authority of the *Brahmans*. The third *Guru* preached equality and instituted the practice of *langar* (free kitchen). With this practice everyone, regardless of religion or caste, could receive a free meal and sit together in a row to eat in the Sikh temple. The fourth and fifth *Gurus* developed the town now known as Amritsar and the Sikh shrine, the 'Golden Temple'. This temple is open to anyone and everyone, irrespective of religion. *Guru* Arjun, the fifth *Guru* (1563-1606), collected the hymns composed by his predecessors and those of Hindu and Muslim saints and added them to his own compositions. This anthology of sacred writings came to be known as *Granth Sahib* and later became the holy scripture of the Sikhs. The martyrdom of *Guru* Arjun was a profound shock to the Sikhs and they began to change from a pacifist to a martial people. Arjun's successor Hargobind wore two swords, *Miri* and *Piri*, signifying the temporal and spiritual aspects of the Sikh faith. The final transformation of the Sikhs into a militant sect came with the last of the ten *Gurus*, *Guru* Gobind Singh, when his father, the ninth *Guru*, was executed. He organised Sikhs into a fighting force, believing that it was righteous to draw the sword when other means fail. He created the *Khalsa* (the pure ones) in 1699 and gave them a common identity.

Sikh women in the survey regard their religion as simple and practical, reflecting the Sikh way of life as laid down in the *Gurus'* teachings. All the women interviewed for this report were devoted to their faith, except for two who said that they did not believe in religion. However, both still attended *gurdwaras* despite their lack of belief. The other women were more positive. One seventy-two-year-old Sikh woman said that religion gave her inner peace. She had had a thriving business but had left worldly affairs and turned to religion. Since then she had felt serene and contented. A thirty-year-old woman stated that religion gave her strength to fight against injustice. A forty-five-year-old woman said that religion disciplined her and taught her how to lead her life properly.

The main sources of Sikh teachings quoted by Sikh women are the sacred scripture of the Sikhs, the *Guru Granth Sahib, Janam-Sakhis* (life stories of *Gurus*) and *Rahit-nama* (the Sikh code of conduct). The *Guru* Granth Sahib is the main religious scripture from which Sikhs draw their inspiration and guidance. The collection was compiled under the supervision of *Guru* Arjun Dev (the fifth *Guru*), by his disciple Bhai Gurdas, a renowned theologian of the time. By commissioning a compilation of the work of the first five *Gurus* at a comparatively early date, he ensured the preservation of the authentic text. This collection was completed in 1604 and is now variously known as the *Adi Granth*, the *Granth Sahib*, or the *Guru Granth Sahib*. It is believed that the last of the *Gurus* decreed that after his death the authority of the *Guru* should pass to the *Guru Granth Sahib*. Every *gurdwara* has a copy of this sacred book installed.

Devout Sikhs often keep a copy of this at home in a separate room specially reserved for religious purposes or they keep *sainchis* (the *Guru Granth Sahib* divided into two volumes, which can be kept on a bookshelf and do not necessarily require a separate room). This text is treated as a *Guru* giving guidance to believers in Sikh teachings. Amongst the women who were interviewed in Leeds for this report, five had the *Granth Sahib* in their homes and a further ten had *sainchis* in their possession. Almost all Sikh homes have the *gutka* (a collection of *gurbani* meant to be read as daily prayers) in one form or another. This does not have to be treated with the same reverence as the Holy Scripture, though it is generally wrapped in a clean cloth and kept carefully on a top shelf, as a sign of respect.

The women also mentioned two other important sources: *Janam-sakhis* and *Rahitnama*. The *Janam-sakhis* contain accounts of the lives of Sikh *Gurus*, and the most important is that of the first *Guru*. They have enjoyed widespread popularity in the *Panth* (sect) and continue to exercise a strong influence on popular beliefs. Some elderly Sikh women told me that they often related stories from this collection to younger members of their family. Sikh children showed me an English version of Sikh stories derived from the *Janam-sakhis* and many of them knew these stories by heart.

Sikh behaviour should be based on the *Rahit* (code of conduct), recorded in a manual called the *Rahitnama*. Sikhs are required to observe the code and practice in their life. According to *Gurmat* (*Guru*'s teachings), there are certain moral, social, religious and ethical principles intrinsic to Sikh beliefs and practices, and it is these that are contained in the *Rahitnama*. The modern 'authorised' version of the Sikh Code of Conduct, the *Rahit Maryada*, has won widespread acceptance as an accurate statement of the *Guru*'s intention. Women in their interviews often quoted this source and most seemed to possess a copy, as it is widely available in English and Punjabi, free of charge from *gurdwaras*. One forty-five-year-old Sikh woman quoted the words of *Guru* Gobind Singh: '*Rahit pyari mujh ko Sikh pyara nahin*' which means that *Rahit* is dearer to the *Guru* than a Sikh, indicating the importance of *Rahit* in the lives of Sikhs.

Women's observance of Sikh teachings

What are the views and practices of Sikh women? Do they adhere to the Sikh teachings and ethos? For comparison, it is essential to explain the normative values of the Sikhs. This will also help reveal what other influences affect their lives.

The opening words of the *Guru Granth Sahib* are *Ik Onkar* (God is one). Sikhism believes in one God who is beyond birth and death, while the worship of idols and the belief in reincarnation of God is unacceptable. As He is formless, He cannot be established or installed as an idol. This one God is known by many names in the *Gurbani* such as *Ram, Gopal, Hari, Nirankar*. However, Sikhs traditionally use two names in worship, and especially in *nam japna* or *namsimran* (the reciting of God's name). These are *Satnam* (*sat* meaning 'true' and *nam* meaning 'name') and *Vaheguru* (meaning 'wonderful Lord'). This survey revealed that many Sikh women were believers and worshippers of one God.

They normally recite the name of God through *namsimran* or by reciting *path* (*Gurbani* – Sikh hymns). They pray at home, attend ladies' *satsangs* and visit *gurdwaras*. Initiated women take a bath early in the morning and recite the five *banis* (passages from *Guru Granth Sahib*) if they are literate in Punjabi. Sikh women who cannot read Punjabi practice *namsimran* in the early hours of the day. Young Sikh women seem less keen on praying because of other demands on their time and also their inability to read the Punjabi language. Two young women told me that they bow in front of their holy book or the photo of their *Gurus*, saying *Satnam Vaheguru* in the morning before leaving for work.

Sikh women also seem emotionally attached to their religion. It was observed during the interviews that most of their homes had pictures of the *Gurus* in their drawing rooms. One woman showed me a framed calendar picture with pride. She said that she was very fortunate to have accidentally found this picture when shopping in the late 1950s as such things were not readily available then. Religious symbols are also used as decoration. In some homes, words or phrases in ornamental *Gurmukhi* script are used as wall plaques and occasionally painted on front doors and on cars. The most common of them is formed from the first two words of the *Guru Granth Sahib: Ik Onkar*. Many women also wear this symbol on a gold chain. Another symbol that features on calendars, books and artifacts is the collection of weapons which appears in black on the yellow *Nishan Sahib*, the banner that flies over every *gurdwara*. It consists of a *Khanda* (a broad, double edged sword) used in the Sikh initiation ceremony (*khande di pahul*), encircled by a *chakri* (a sharp-edged steel discus), and flanked by two crossed *tilwars* (scimitars).

Some Sikh women, particularly the middle-aged and elderly from rural backgrounds, do worship more than one God, although this is condemned by the Sikh religion. 'They, who wave in their Faith and know not their Lord, worship the gods and goddesses of stone' (*Adi Granth*: 332). During the survey, I found Sikh women in the *Radhasoami, Nirankari* and *Baba Vishvakarma satsangs*, who are not Sikh in essence. They attend the Hindu temple to appease the *devi mata* (goddess). They also believe in deities, *murtipuja* (deity worship) and supernatural powers and go to other places of worship. I asked some women the reason for their belief in multiple deities and their reply was that God could be worshipped in any form (*rab nun manana kite vi hovey*). This attitude seems to be more common in families where Hindus and Sikhs are married to one another. It may also be the influence of social interaction with other religions, together with an ignorance of true Sikh religious teachings.

The worship of supernatural powers, ghosts and evil influences is not permitted in the Sikh religion (*Rahitnama*, 1992:17). Some Sikh women in this survey were found, however, to believe in black magic (*dhaga taveet*), healer *sants* and sorcerers (*jadu tuna de mantar paran wala*). This may be the influence of Punjabi folk traditions and social norms of the Punjab, which have affected Sikh religious values.

Image worship is also common. Most *gurdwaras* have photographs of Sikh *Gurus*, especially *Guru* Nanak and *Guru* Gobind Singh, hung in the main prayer hall. It is not unusual to see in Sikh homes the photographs of Sikh *Gurus*, saints and Hindu deities coexisting happily with coloured posters of film stars. These observations were most useful as an indication of common religious perceptions, suggesting that although Sikhs have faith in the spiritual traditions of Punjab, they see nothing wrong in having such pictures hanging together. It is also a reflection of practices that are far removed from the orthodox Sikh religion.

Family life

Sikh teachings stress the importance of family life. It is recommended in Sikhism that one can best lead a pious life while living within a family. Renunciation or celibacy is discarded in favour of family life in the Sikh religion. 'Why go out to search God in the woods? For, though ever Detached, He abides within us all: Yea, He also lives within thee' (*Adi Granth*: 684). Family life is very important to the women interviewed for this report. They strongly believe in the institution of marriage and looking after their families. They also believe in *karma da phal* (the results of their good or evil deeds) and *chaurasi lakh jaun* (transmigration of the soul through the cycle of birth and death) which provide a strong incentive for them to do good deeds. Such beliefs also encourage them to control negative desires such as lust, greed and pride in order to lead a pious and contented family life.

Sikh traditions
Sikh traditions emphasise *seva* (voluntary service), sharing with the less fortunate, *sangat* (congregation), *pangat* (sitting in a row), *langar* (communal lunch), equality, *kirt karo* (earning your living through honest and approved means) and *bhana manana* (accepting the will of God).

Seva
Seva (rendering voluntary service for the welfare of humanity) is highly valued in the Sikh religion. The ideal of a true Sikh is to look beyond the self and to serve fellow beings. Sikh women generally observe the practice of *seva* and perform it without promoting their own interests. *Seva* can be interpreted in a number of ways, such as looking after one's parents, contributing to charities and carrying out voluntary service in the community and *gurdwaras*. The most common *seva* performed by Sikh women is to work in the community kitchen, prepare *langar* (communal food), clean the kitchen and other parts of the *gurdwara* as an obligation of their religious duty. Almost all the Sikh women I spoke to feel privileged to do *seva* in *langar*. In addition to serving in the community kitchen, some taught music, the Punjabi language and *gurbani* (religious hymns) in the *gurdwaras*.

Sharing with the less fortunate
Sharing with the less fortunate includes giving money to the needy and sharing food with the poor and hungry. Sikh religious teachings recommend giving *daswandh* (one tenth of earnings to charity) for good causes. Sikh families regularly donate money towards *langar*, the maintenance of *gurdwaras*, charities and other humane causes. Sikh women in this country are wage earners and they donate generously towards *gurdwara* funds. A few Sikh women told me that they had donated substantial amounts from their first pay packets, on the birth of their son, at the time of a wedding or a celebration of other occasions such as getting a job, promotion or buying a house. They also donate to people suffering natural disasters such as floods and earthquakes. This was evident from the collections made by Sikh women for the sufferers of the earthquake in Gujarat in India despite tensions in Hindu-Sikh relations. According to their religious teachings Sikhs are obliged to offer food to the poor and hungry, known as

wand chhakna. Sikh women are keen to do so, believing that someone needy may be God visiting you in human form. One woman told me that her mother-in-law advised her to make extra food in case a hungry person came in search of food. Another woman told me that her mother made her go without, but did not deny food to a hungry woman. *Namdhari* Sikhs are very particular about *daswandh.*

Congregation

From the time of *Guru* Nanak, some important institutions developed that still continue today. One such institution is the *sangat,* or congregation. *Guru* Nanak encouraged a congregational style of spirituality, keeping shrines open to people of all castes and creeds without any discrimination. Wherever Sikhs go, they try to build a *gurdwara* so that they can meet and hold *diwan* and *kirtan* (hymn singing). This serves a dual purpose. Firstly, it provides a meeting place for religious-minded people and secondly, it serves as a centre for religious discussion and preaching. A Sikh is required to keep *sangat* (the company of noble souls), for in such company the mind is purified. Sikhs place a great deal of importance on *sangat,* believing that sitting in the *sangat* with other devotees helps to develop humility, love, equality, fraternity and brotherhood. Sikh women make every effort to attend the congregation. One fifty-year-old woman said, 'I feel that I am missing something if I do not go to the *gurdwara* and sit in the *sangat'.* Another woman said that she learned a lot about her religion by attending the *gurdwara.* Another forty-year-old woman said that attending the congregation was useful not only for religious purposes but also for her social life.

Pangat and Langar

Another institution of huge importance is *pangat* (row) and *Guru Ka Langar* (free kitchen). The free kitchen laid the foundation of equality. It is essential for the *langar* takers to sit in a *pangat* without any distinction between caste, creed, religion or social status. *Langar* has become

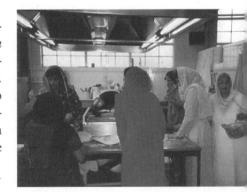

Preparation of Langar

a unique and integral part of Sikh life. Sikhs donate generously towards *langar* and women take pride in *langar seva*. All *gurdwaras* in Britain provide a free *langar* on Sundays. On important occasions, Sikh families organise *langar* and invite all their relations, friends, acquaintances and members of the congregation. In Britain, *langar* is not only for the needy and poor, but for all the members of the congregation who attend the service. One elderly Sikh woman commented that *langar* was a unique practice started by the *Gurus*. Another forty-nine-year-old woman said that the practice of *langar* combined *seva* and sharing food with others. One young woman remarked, 'We are away from our families and relations in a foreign land. It is good to organise *langar* in order to celebrate and share your happiness with others'. One thirty-year-old woman said that this was the best way to put the teachings on equality into practice.

Equality

Equality is a key concept in the Sikh religion with regard to caste, class and gender. The teachings of Sikhism categorically reject using the caste system as a pretext for promoting inequality. There is no place for divisions based on caste, for no man is born high or low. According to *Guru* Amardas,

> All say there are four castes
> But God creates one and all...
> The five elements make up the body
> And nobody can say who has less or more.
> (*Adi Granth*: 1128)

Guru Gobind Singh declared caste to be a hindrance to the brotherhood of the *Khalsa* and to ensure equality he instituted the practice of adding 'Singh' to the names of all Sikh men and 'Kaur' to those of Sikh women. This is significant for Sikhs as these names bring them within the fold of the *Khalsa Panth*. Sikhs are also instructed not to use their caste as part of their names, but in England many attach their caste, *gotra*, or clan name (such as Channa, Cheema, Sethi) to their given names, because the use of a surname is a requirement in the UK. The Sikh community has not thought of any alternative to the use of surnames that would still safeguard their religious traditions. The other reason for this continued practice is that here the caste system is deeply ingrained within the Sikh community and finding an alternative is not seen to be necessary. It is unfortunate that in England even caste-based *gurdwaras* may be found.

The Sikh religion promotes a classless society, giving more importance to virtue than wealth. The status of an individual should be determined by deeds or merits and not by class position. All should be treated as equal, irrespective of their material resources. *Guru* Arjun Dev said, 'The wisdom of God looks upon all alike, such as the wind that blows alike for the commoner and the king' (*Adi Granth*: 272). However, as the community is becoming more settled and established in Britain, a class system has gradually emerged. Sikh women are experiencing the growing impact of this hierarchy which further divides the community on economic lines, for instance, businessmen, doctors, public sector workers or manual workers. This is reflected in the associations and organisations set up by different classes of Sikhs. For example, there are associations which are mainly for doctors and businessmen. Sikh parents also favour certain occupations for their sons and daughters, such as medicine, dentistry, law or engineering, so that their family's social status may improve. One woman in the survey felt that class would soon take preference over caste.

The Sikh concept of equality applies naturally to both men and women in secular and religious life and is promoted through the teachings and practices of the *Gurus*. Sikhism advocates sex equality and accords women an equal place in society. At the emergence of Sikhism, the *Gurus* condemned practices prevalent in the fifteenth century which undermined women, such as the veiling of women, *sati* and female infanticide. Sikhism allowed widows to remarry and *Guru* Nanak condemned the custom of wearing the veil. In India, *sati* and infanticide were only legally abolished in the nineteenth century. Sikh teachings also give women full equality to participate in religious performances, to be equal partners in marriage and family life and, if the need arises, to participate in warfare.

Most of my informants felt that they were better off than many other Asian women but still not exactly equal with men. They told me that they were equal in terms of taking part in religious performances but not in the management of religious institutions. One fifty-year-old woman said, 'Most Sikh temples are male-dominated. Most committee members are male'. When investigating this with some committee members of *gurdwaras*, I was told that women were not coming forward and that they could not afford to spend the time required in the management of *gurdwaras*. Some women informants did not agree with this view, which they claimed was biased. In some *gurdwaras* women were not allowed to read the *Guru Granth Sahib*. When I inquired about the reason for this, a very prominent person told me that they were not against women reading *Guru Granth Sahib*. He explained in detail that it was a local practice rather than a religious dictate. 'The changeover of *granthis* (readers of the Holy book) in *Akhand path* often results in bodily contact, which is not approved of in our organisation. However, there is no restriction for women to organise women-only *Akhand path*'. The decisions made by *gurdwaras* seemed to lack a female perspective. One informant laughed and said, 'We are used as cooks to prepare *langar* and cleaners to clean the communal kitchen. On our strength *gurdwaras* run but we are not part of any decision-making. The only women who are allowed to come forward are the wives and the relatives of executive committee members'.

Another informant told me, 'It is a pity that the males dominating the *gurdwaras* are modestly educated and lack organisational and management ability and skills. They do not involve women and young Sikhs, especially educated ones, as they feel threatened'.

Some women, who had the time and desire to serve the community felt frustrated by the behaviour of the *gurdwara*'s power holders. Others had found a way through ladies' *satsangs* to make their voice heard in *gurdwaras*. A thirty-two-year-old active member of a ladies' *satsang* group stated that the management committee of their *gurdwara* needed to listen to them if they wanted to keep on receiving their donations.

Men, therefore, still dominate Sikh religious institutions. Women are largely invisible, or at least marginal to the public positions of power, authority and hierarchy. Sikhism, in spite of giving full equality to women, has not in practice been able to create a more equal and just situation between women and men. One woman commented that even today men take pleasure in undermining women. She feels that Sikh men think that women are incapable of providing academic work. One female writer told me her story. 'I produced two poetry books and took them to *gurdwaras* to publicise them. I requested the secretary to make an announcement at the end of *diwan*, which he did not. They did nothing for me but made a mockery of me.' She felt ridiculed and humiliated and was furious about the whole incident. This was not an isolated incident but reflective of the general experience of many women. A sixty-five-year-old woman said that Sikh men should be conscious that Sikh women would not tolerate this situation much longer. One young woman said, 'It is the women who are the makers of the future generation and are the first teachers of their children, and also instil religious belief in them. It is not fair that they are not involved in taking active decisions affecting themselves and their children.'

Kirt karo

Sikh belief in *kirt karo* (earning a living by honest and approved means) has had a significant impact on Sikh women. Sikh women have a strong work ethos. They do not like to beg or ask for financial help, even when they are in difficult circumstances. One Sikh woman in her early forties told me that she was widowed when her children were still young. She was illiterate and it was hard for her to get a job. She sewed clothes for women and from those earnings she looked after her family. She did not ask her relatives for help, nor did she apply for social security or other benefits, believing that these were charitable handouts. There was a common belief among early migrants that social security was charity, which Sikhs would not accept. The early migrant women in the survey looked for work even when they could not speak English. Later, when they felt the need to watch their grown-up daughters, they opened shops in their homes.

Accepting the will of God

Many Sikh women in the survey believed in God's will (*tera bhana mitha lagay*) which should be accepted without complaint or questioning. Within Sikhism, a person should remain the same in happiness and grief, believing that everything happens according to the will of God (*Guru da bhana*). This belief seems to have strengthened amongst Sikh women in recent years. They accept many things by saying that it is *hony* or *sanjog* (divine order). Many Sikh women used to cry loudly when someone died, but it is now more common to hear *Guru da bhana*. One woman said that her husband died of cancer when she was only twenty-eight.

She did not cry, but accepted the will of God, saying that she had looked after him and given him all the happiness she could.

Sikh identity

Sikhs were given their identity by the tenth *Guru*, Gobind Singh. He created the initiation ceremony and the Sikh symbols. In order to become a complete Sikh, one has to undergo an initiation ceremony and keep the Sikh symbols (the five *K*s), which give a unique and easily recognised external identity.

Amrit Pahul (Initiation)

One is not born a Sikh, but acquires that status by following Sikh teachings and undergoing the specifically religious rite of *amrit chhakna* or initiation. Initiation into the Sikh *panth* was originally by *charanamrit* (amrit from the feet), received from the *Guru* himself from the days of *Guru* Nanak until 1699. *Guru* Gobind Singh, the tenth *Guru* of the Sikhs, replaced *charanamrit* with *Khande ka Amrit* (*Amrit Pahul*) and created a *Khalsa* with a distinctive identity. He chose his five beloved ones from amongst the congregation. They each belonged to different castes and merged together into the *Khalsa* brotherhood, which aimed to create a society of equals. They were then initiated and were given a common identity supported by the five *K*s. This was also the time at which 'Singh' and 'Kaur' were added to Sikh names.

Formal initiation into the Sikh faith is traditionally one of the most important and sacred ceremonies of Sikhism. In the past, it was not commonly performed in Britain. With the time and efforts of some committed Sikhs, it is now on the increase. One prominent Sikh told me that the number of Sikhs, including women, interested in undergoing the initiation ceremony was increasing every year. There are more initiated elderly women now whereas initiation is less popular among young Sikh women. Some women in the survey said that it was a good thing to be initiated, but that it should not be forced upon young people, 'Let them come forward when they are ready'. Nonetheless, initiated Sikh women are proud of their status and of their identity as *amritdharis*.

This initiation is seen as the way to spiritual development, when coupled with adherence to the ethical principles of Sikhism. The ceremony is for women as well as men and takes place at an age when the person can understand its significance. Taking *amrit* is an expression of commitment for a Sikh. Five Sikh men or women can perform this rite. Both outwardly and inwardly they should represent the perfection of a Sikh. As long as the place where the ceremony is held is one where there is a certain amount of privacy, there is no restriction upon the location or on the number of people taking part. An initiated Sikh should adhere to the five *K*s, be tidily dressed and openly attempt to follow the Sikh way of life as well as accept the doctrines of Sikhism. I was told that although women may be initiated, it is normal that men conduct the ceremony and so far there has been no participation of any woman. A more comprehensive account of this initiation ceremony may be found in Cole and Sambhi's *The Sikhs: Their Religious Beliefs and Practices* (1978).

There are also *sahajdhari* Sikhs, who believe in the teachings of *Gurus*, but are not initiated and do not maintain an external identity by wearing or using the outward symbols of Sikhism. There are also Sikhs who keep a beard, uncut hair and wear a turban but are not initiated. They are referred to as *keshadhari* Sikhs. These distinctions, even though applied to men, are also applicable to women, particularly in the current situation where many women have their hair cut and trimmed.

The five *K*s

The initiated Sikhs wear the five articles of faith commonly known as 'the five *K*s' (*panj kakke* or *kakar*). *Guru* Gobind Singh gave Sikhs an identity in the form of five symbols, all beginning with the letter *K*. For the bearers, it is an indication of their allegiance to the *Khalsa Panth*. The symbols are *kes* (uncut hair), *kangha* (comb), *kirpan* (dagger), *kachha* (undergarment) and *kara* (steel bangle). Sikh women adhere to the five *K*s if they have taken *amrit*. Non-*amritdhari* middle-aged and older Sikh women have uncut hair and wear *kachha* and a *kara*. Some younger Sikh women only maintain two of the *K*s by not cutting their hair and by wearing *kara*. It is important to consider the significance of the five *K*s as perceived by Sikh women.

Sikh women over forty-five years of age believed *Kes* (uncut hair) to be very important. They told me that it was against their religion to cut their hair. It was their duty to preserve and maintain the things that God had given them. A Sikh woman of fifty said that uncut head and body hair was symbolic of an acceptance of God's will. It was also considered to be a sign of spiritual and moral strength. Despite this, there is a growing trend among young Sikh women to cut their hair. In this survey, I found that many young women had their hair cut in order to follow fashion. I asked one Sikh woman in her forties, who belonged to a religious family, the reasons for trimming her hair. She told me that she had seen a hairstyle in a magazine which had taken her fancy and she had copied it. Other informants told me that they did not believe in following religious dictates and they were Sikhs only by birth. A few women said that they stood out as looking different if they had long hair. Some women pointed out that they should not be asked to keep uncut hair when male members of the household were clean-shaven. Most of the young women cut or trim their hair, including women from *keshadhari* families. I asked one twenty-two-year-old woman, 'How it is possible for you to have your hair trimmed when your father is so strict?' Her answer was that her father did not like it but reluctantly allowed her just to trim her hair rather than having it cut short. One eighteen-year-old girl said that she wanted to have her hair cut but she was scared of her parents' reaction. It seems that parents have relaxed traditions so that they can maintain a good relationship with their daughters. The cutting of hair also indicates a strong western influence and the influence of Indian Bollywood films.

Sikh women are aware of the importance of the *Kangha* (a small comb) in the Sikh religion. They stated that it was a symbol of personal care and cleanliness, orderly spirituality and discipline of the mind. Some Sikh women said that they always kept a small comb in their handbag. Other non-*amritdhari* women also tied a *kangha* in their hair to maintain the tradition.

Sikh women also know the significance of the *Kirpan* (dagger) and explain it as a symbol of resistance against evil. The *kirpan* is a symbol of freedom from oppression and servility. It signifies dignity and self-respect. Its obvious meaning is of self-defence and individual freedom. The sword, in the mind, cuts at the roots of ignorance, evil and worldly attachment and destroys them utterly. *Guru* Gobind Singh justified the use of the sword when all methods of peaceful negotiation for seeking justice failed. Similarly, women understand the importance of *Kachha*, an undergarment and symbol of chastity. This also signifies modesty, moral restraint and continence. These two *K*s are worn almost exclusively by *amritdhari* Sikhs. Drury conducted similar research in Nottingham on the maintenance of religious traditions among young Sikhs and came to similar conclusions on the use of *kachha* and *kirpan* (1988: 390).

The *Kara* is a steel bangle, a symbol of responsibility and allegiance to God. It is worn on the right wrist, reminding Sikhs that God is eternal with no beginning and no end. Most Sikh women, young and old, wear a *kara*, especially when visiting the *gurdwara*.

Sikh rites and ceremonies

The Sikh ceremonies for birth, marriage and death have a special significance for the Sikh community and are closely associated with religion. These ceremonies are performed in the *gurdwara* in the presence of family, relatives and friends.

Birth

Religion is an integral part of Sikh life, from birth until death. The birth of any child, boy or girl, should be taken as a blessing and gift from God. When a child is born, a naming ceremony is held in the *gurdwara* a few weeks after its birth. Nearly all children receive their name in this traditional manner. After a prayer from the family, the name of the child is taken from the first letter of the *vak* (the first word of the passage of the *Guru Granth Sahib* read after its random opening) from the left-hand page and this is read to the parents. They will then decide upon a name beginning with the first letter and the *granthi* will announce it publicly, adding Kaur for a girl or Singh for a boy. Sikhs add a 'surname' while registering the birth of their child. The surname is inherited patrilineally (from the father) and is usually derived from the village of origin, the *gotra* or the *jati*. As previously mentioned, this is against Sikh religious tenets because of its caste associations. Quite often, the child is later given an anglicised nickname either by parents or by playmates. I did not find a single woman who had not taken her child to a *gurdwara* for a naming ceremony. The women told me that the naming ceremony was most important for Sikh children and in most cases, this was the first visit at which the child and the family received religious blessings.

Marriage

The Sikh marriage is known as *Anand karaj* (*Anand* meaning bliss and *karaj* meaning ceremony). In Sikhism, marriage is not viewed simply as a social and civil contract, but is seen as a spiritual state, since family life is central to the Sikh way of life. The marriage ceremony (*Anand karaj*) takes place in the *gurdwara* before midday and involves *lavan* (the recitation of four stanzas from the *Guru Granth Sahib*) in the presence of the bride, the bridegroom and their relatives and friends. The groom comes forward and takes his place at the front of the *Adi Granth*. The bride then joins the congregation and sits at the left side of the groom, attended by a sister, sister-in-law or a friend. Whoever is conducting the marriage then asks the couple and their parents to stand whilst he or she prays that God will bless the marriage. The bride and groom publicly assent to the marriage by bowing towards the *Guru Granth Sahib*. When they sit down, the bride's father performs the *palla frowna* ceremony (he ties the end of his daughter's *dupatta* to the muslin scarf which hangs from the groom's shoulders). The officiant then opens the *Guru Granth Sahib* and the *lavan* (marriage verses) are read, and then sung by the *ragis* (religious musicians) as the couple walk slowly round the *Guru Granth Sahib* in a clockwise direction. This happens four times. The last time is often a signal for the throwing of flower petals. The service concludes with the singing of the first five and the last stanzas of the *Anand*, followed by the prayer, *ardas* and *vak*. The ceremony concludes with advice on the institution of marriage and its importance in life from a knowledgeable person from the Sikh community. After the religious ceremony, other celebrations take place at the bride's home, in a hall or at a hotel. Finally, the marriage party and the bride depart (*doli*) for the groom's home in the late afternoon.

Namdhari Sikhs marry according to *vedi viah* (a Hindu custom where the bride and the bridegroom sit in front of the holy fire), which includes reading *lavan* from the *Guru Granth Sahib*. They believe that all the Sikh *Gurus* were married according to *vedi viah*. For a *vedi*, a place is first marked off with four upright stakes joined by cross-pieces of wood at the top and the inside. This is covered with a red cloth called a *vedi*. Alternatively, they prepare a *havan kund* (a large steel vessel for the sacred fire) and install the *Guru Granth Sahib*. Five *Namdhari* Sikhs prepare *amrit*, as the bride and bridegroom must be initiated before the wedding. Seven *Namdhari* Sikhs recite *gurbani* and perform the *havan* ceremony. The bride and bridegroom walk round the *havan kund* four times in an anti-clockwise direction, while the *lavas* are read from the *Guru Granth Sahib*. *Havan*, according to the *Namdharis*, signifies that the couple promise not to part until death.

Sikh weddings normally take place in the *gurdwara* according to Sikh *Rahit Maryada*. Some *gurdwaras* do not perform mixed marriages between Sikhs and non-Sikhs. A woman whose daughter was getting married to a *gora* (a term used for a white man) told me that her daughter insisted on being married according to the Sikh religion, so she had arranged the marriage in a hotel as it could not be performed in a *gurdwara*. Another Sikh woman told me that she had wanted to marry a *gora* and had begged her mother to give her a Sikh religious wedding, to which her mother did not agree. In the end, her in-laws had given her a Sikh religious wedding. This is an indication of the high value placed by Sikh women on a religious wedding, irrespective of the nature of the partnership.

The re-marriage of widows is permitted in Sikhism and the marriage is performed in more or less the same manner. I was told that the marriage ceremony is different in traditional families where *lavan* will not be performed, as the bride is not a virgin. One fifty-five-year-old woman told me that in the Punjab, widows did not go through the same ceremony, but underwent a simple rite of *chadar pauna* (offering protection), a Punjabi custom rather than a Sikh one.

Death

Sikhs believe in *bhana manana* (accepting the will of God) and see death as part of the natural life cycle. Sikhs should not cry when someone dies but should remember the name of God (*namsimran*) and pray for the dead. At death, Sikhs cremate the body. They share the view of many inhabitants of hot climates that the funeral should take place quickly, normally on the day of death. This practice is followed in the Punjab and the dead are cremated before sunset on the same day. If someone dies after sunset, that person is cremated as soon as possible the next day.

The Sikh religion is against the custom of transferring a dead body from the bed to the ground, placing a lighted lamp on its hand and then wailing and lamenting for the departed. Sikhism also condemns *pitt siapa* (women hitting different parts of their body with their hands) and saying *vayen* (to lament by recounting the virtues of a deceased person).

> They cry 'alas, alas', and wail for the dead. They beat their cheeks and pull out their hair. Did they but cherish the name and practice it. Nanak, it would be a sacrifice for them (*Adi Granth*:1410).

Despite religious teachings, it is a common practice in the Punjab to carry out *pitt siapa* when someone dies. I found through observation that many Sikh families in England still continue this tradition. I asked one Sikh woman the reason for *pitt siapa*. She said that it was natural to cry when someone dear to you dies. I asked another woman who was not related to the deceased the reason for her crying and she replied that it was a custom. This suggests that *pitt siapa* is a tradition of showing affection for the dead whether or not the dead person is known or related to one.

The cremation ceremony is a family occasion. The dead body is washed and clothed by members of the family, who ensure that the symbols of the faith are worn. In the Punjab, the body is then taken to the cremation ground outside the village. In England, it is brought home in a coffin and the family members pray for the soul. The coffin is then taken to the *gurdwara*, where other acquaintances and friends pray for the deceased's soul. From the *gurdwara*, it proceeds to the crematorium. At the crematorium, a *granthi* (Sikh priest) leads the mourners in the reading of *Kirtan Sohilla* from the *Guru Granth Sahib*, and this is followed by *ardas*. Traditionally, it was the eldest son who lit the funeral pyre. In England, an electric switch is pressed. The ashes and bones are consigned to running water. Most Sikhs take the ashes to India and consign them at Anandpur (Punjab).

In England, both men and women attend the funeral. It is normal to return to the *gurdwara*, where congregations wash their hands and faces (a custom brought from the Punjab, where it is necessary to wash, as ashes can fall on them because of the burning of the body out in the open). I noted that many young women followed this tradition by copying their elders. It is then customary for the complete reading of the *Guru Granth* to begin, although on this occasion it is more likely to be done inter- mittently over a period of about ten days. For the last few years, the reading has started as soon as someone dies and the *bhog* (the ceremony performed on the completion of the reading of the *Guru Granth Sahib*) takes place after the funeral, which allows relatives living away to attend the whole event. Before taking leave of the bereaved family, mourners are served food. It has be- come the responsibility of the *gurdwara* to serve food to all the mourners on the day of the funeral. Sikh women help the mourning family by preparing *langar*. The sharing of food at this time is particularly meaningful. It symbolises the continuity of social life and normal activities, as opposed to isolation from human contacts, fasting and other ritual manifestations of grief.

Death is the removal of the last obstacle to complete union with God. It is common for *Guru* Arjun's *Sukhmani* (hymn of peace) or a similar *shabad* to be read in the presence of the dying person. One elderly woman told me that the period of mourning usually lasted ten days. During this time relatives and friends come home to give their condolences and to pay their respects to the dead. Relatives will usually make gifts to the poor, to the *gurdwara* or to a charity. I have noted that clothes, bedding, utensils and money are given to the *gurdwara* and donations to charities by the family of the deceased. The erection of memorials and hold- ing a *sharadh* ceremony (feeding Brahmans to honour dead ancestors) are not allowed in Sikhism. Sikhs in England normally follow this teaching and do not erect memorials, but I was told that some traditional families perform *sharadh* every year.

Gurdwaras

The place for Sikh religious worship is called a *gurdwara*. A *gurd- wara* is the house of the *Guru*, where the *Guru* (in the form of *Guru Granth Sahib*) himself resides. The Sikh religion is a con- gregational religion and Sikhs believe that the *Guru* is manifested in *sangat*. The *Gurus* made it clear that attendance at communal worship is a necessary part of the spiritual life of a Sikh:

> *Sat Sangat* (the Holy Congregation) is the school of the True
> *Guru*
> There we learn to love him and appreciate his greatness.
> (*Var Kanra, mohalla* 4: 1299)

Gurdwaras are communal places of worship. In England, the weekly *diwan* is held on Sunday. This is an assembly for the purposes of worship, receiving religious instruction and discussing matters of communal interest. In weekly *diwans*, there is a recitation from the *Guru Granth Sahib*, *kirtan*, *ardas* and *vak*. In addition to normal prayers and *kirtan*, there is also *katha* and *viakhia* (explanation of religious traditions) by *granthis*. Some Sikh women want to learn about their religion in depth and they take a keen interest in *katha* and *viakhia*. *Karah prasad* (a mixture of clarified butter, flour and sugar) is distributed and *langar* (communal lunch) is served. Sikh families are likely to attend the *gurdwara* on a Sunday if they are not doing anything else such as visiting relatives or attending weddings. Attendance at the *gurdwara* is generally high for major festivals and *gurupurbs* (anniversaries of *Gurus*). Most *gurdwaras* remain open every day of the week and some Sikhs go to the *gurdwara* daily.

A copy of the *Guru Granth Sahib* is installed in the *gurdwara* and is opened, read and closed every day with great respect. It is kept under a canopy and the *chauri* (which consists of yak tail hair or artificial fibre set in a wooden or metal holder) is waved over the sacred book as a sign of respect. All Sikh rituals are conducted in the presence of the *Guru Granth Sahib*. Both men and women may read the *Guru Granth Sahib* if they have competence in *Gurmukhi* and both men and women may officiate at Sikh ceremonies.

Gurdwaras are well established in England but they differ in nature and organisation. The *Gurdwara* is open to the public and can be visited by any person, from any religion, sex and caste, although caste-based *gurdwaras* can be found here, which are generally attended by Sikhs from those castes. A *granthi* or *bhai* (priest) acts as the caretaker, and is also skilled in reciting *gurbani* and *kirtan* (hymn singing). It has been observed that all the *granthis* are male although most *gurdwaras* have a women's group who perform *kirtan* on Sundays and hold a ladies' *satsang* once a week. The *gurdwaras* depend on voluntary *seva* (service) and the main source of their income is the donations and voluntary contributions made by Sikhs when bowing in front of the *Guru Granth Sahib*. Sikh women also make generous donations from their income and pensions.

Sikhs attend the *gurdwara* as a family. On entering the hall, Sikh worshippers kneel, touching the floor with their foreheads before the *Guru Granth Sahib* and make their offerings of money. Some people also offer flowers, sugar, milk or fruit. Everybody sits on the floor of the prayer hall, women on one side and men on the other side. *Namdhari* Sikhs do not keep the *Guru Granth Sahib* under the canopy but make an *asan* (seat) for it. For them the *Guru Granth Sahib* is only a sacred *granth* and not a *Guru*. They keep a large photo of *Satguru Ram Singh* in the main hall and they bow in front of him.

Before entering the prayer hall, as a mark of respect shoes must be removed and the head must be covered. In *gurdwaras*, large handkerchiefs are available for those who do not have anything with which to cover their heads. According to Sikh teachings, dress should be modest. One devout Sikh woman, commenting on modest dress, said that the *gurdwara* had become a place for a fashion show and that some women came in wearing low necklines, sleeveless tops and transparent sleeves and headscarves. No smoking and no drinking of alcohol is permitted anywhere in the *gurdwara*, nor should tobacco or alcohol be taken into the *gurdwara*, according to Sikh traditions. One young woman said that some men, especially from the management committees, attended *gurdwaras* after having had a drink, which was against the Sikh ethos. She pointed out that the management of *gurdwaras* should be in the hands of pious Sikhs, who would set an example for younger Sikhs.

The *gurdwara* is not only a place of worship but also a centre for religious education. All major functions are held in the *gurdwara* and it is also a source of networking and information for Sikhs. Other activities also take place there, for instance, Punjabi classes, music classes and social activities such as youth clubs, women's groups, welfare provision and day centres for the elderly. In keeping with the Sikh tradition of *seva*, *gurdwaras* often provide temporary accommodation and food for those in need.

Gurdwaras attract a congregation of mainly middle-aged and elderly women. Some young Sikh women attend but the number is not as great. Many young Sikh informants told me that the main activities in *gurdwaras* are conducted in Punjabi and it is difficult for them to understand what is being said. One sixteen-year-old Sikh girl said that she would like to know more about the Sikh religion. However, she had been mocked rather than accepted in the *gurdwara*, as she had cut her hair and went to clubs. It is a general feeling of many young Sikh women that *gurdwaras* are not sympathetic to their problems and their parents cannot explain religious traditions to them logically. There is little provision for young Sikhs, apart from classes in Punjabi and music, which both attract reasonable attendance. *Gurdwaras* attempt to introduce other activities such as mixed *gatka* (martial art) and archery classes for young Sikhs in order to bring them closer to the *gurdwaras*.

The majority of young Sikh women in England, especially those born here, have little or no understanding of the fundamentals of their religion. The language of the *Guru Granth Sahib* is archaic and difficult to understand without an interpreter, especially where it relates to important but complex ideas. There is hardly any facility for religious education, in the sense of explaining the religious and moral teachings of *Gurus* and historical facts in simple English. Consequently, there has been an emphasis on 'symbolic' Sikhism, such as having long hair and other outward signs of Sikh identity. This is also probably the reason that younger women are unable to distinguish between social and religious traditions or accept traditions as passed on to them by older women. Some Sikh girls told me that they looked on the Internet if they needed any information on Sikhism. Another girl told me that she had learnt more about Sikhism in her religious education class at school than elsewhere.

Most Sikh women surveyed for this report believed that the *gurdwaras* were doing a good job. They said that they learnt more about their religion each time they went to the *gurdwara*. Young Sikh women felt happy about the role and contribution of *gurdwaras*, except for their reservation about the lack of religious classes in English. One Sikh woman said that she had not learnt anything about religion when she was young as there had been no proper *gurdwara*. Now she knew about festivals, *gurupurbs* and other important things about her religion, which was all due to the teachings of the *gurdwara*. A thirty-seven-year-old Sikh woman said, 'Sikh children also go to *gurdwaras* and observe how to behave in the community. They learn Punjabi and music, as most *gurdwaras* hold these classes'. Women socialise in the *gurdwara* and learn from each other.

However, despite approving of the *gurdwaras*, almost all the women expressed their frustration with their management and the fights going on within the management committees. One woman commented, 'The management committees in the *gurdwaras* have no respect for anyone. They fight for their ego and power. If they believe in *seva*, this should not happen. There is no sense of justice and equality in them'.

Another women said that *gurdwaras* had divided the Sikh community and created negative feelings in younger people. One young informant said very angrily, 'How dare they criticise us, when they do not observe the Sikh Code of Conduct in their lives? They drink, they cut their hair and they do things which cannot be approved by Sikhism. They are creating divisions instead of doing something constructive for the younger generation'.

I discussed this view with Sikhs who held positions of management in the *gurdwara*. They felt that the main reasons of dissension and conflict were caste divisions within the Sikh community, a lack of consistency of ground rules in running *gurdwaras*, competition among *gurdwaras*, the strong hold of families and groups on the management committees, a lack of committed volunteers and intolerance of constructive criticism.

Some rules of Sikhism have been waived by *gurdwaras* in order to attract *sangat*. For example, worshipping other gods or placing anything on the same level as the *Guru Granth Sahib* are both against Sikh religious tenets. However, a group of Sikh women was allowed by a *gurdwara* management committee to keep the photograph of their local saint at the side of *Guru Granth Sahib* when celebrating his anniversary. On similar lines, there is another group, devotees of *Baba* Vishvakarma (the god of craft and building skills), set up by the Hindu *biradari* of the *Ramgarhia* caste from a particular village who, in the absence of their own venue, initially wanted to meet in *gurdwaras*, with a view to increasing their membership. I was told by a member of a *gurdwara* management committee that sometimes they gave in to such requests in order to retain *sangat*, even though they knew that these are against Sikh religious tenets. A highly-educated woman from Birmingham said that there were too many *gurdwaras* attended by small sections of the Sikh community and some of these difficulties could be overcome if there were fewer *gurdwaras* attended by a wider public.

Sikh women are of the opinion that there is poor management in *gurdwaras*, no recognition of the potential of Sikh women, no sense of delegation, a low literacy level among management committee members and a misuse of power. In response to the issue of there being few committed volunteers, two women in the survey commented that there were many capable retired women in the Sikh community, but the problem with management committees was that all paid positions were kept within certain families or acquaintances and voluntary work done by others was not even acknowledged. Another woman remarked, 'It is a pity that the Sikh community, in spite of being educated and forward looking, has failed to organise a pressure group which could look after their religious, social and cultural interests. They do not realise that they fail to exert any pressure for strategic posts within the council and health authorities and this will eventually affect the future of their children'.

Pilgrimage

Pilgrimage is disapproved of in the Sikh religion and the *Gurus* frequently referred to this custom as a wasted effort:

> Shall we go to bathe at the pilgrim-places?
> No, *Nam* is the only sacred place of pilgrimage.
> The Holy of Holies is the contemplation of the Word
> that gives inner light and spiritual illumination'
> (*Rag Dhanasari, mahalla, Adi Granth*: 687, tr. Ranbir Singh,
> *The Sikh Way of Life*: 17)

However, many Sikh women subscribe to the practice of *gurdwarian de darshan* (visiting or making pilgrimages to particularly holy *gurdwaras*). The five *gurdwaras* in the Indian sub-continent associated with important events in the lives of the *Gurus* (known as the five *takhts*) are visited by devout Sikhs. The most important are the *Darbar Sahib* (the Golden Temple) and the *Akal Takht* in Amritsar. Most Sikhs will try to visit these at least once in their lifetime. There are many other historically significant places for example, *Nankana Sahib* (Talwandi) in Pakistan, the birthplace of *Guru* Nanak; *Keshgarh Sahib* (Anandpur), the place where the *Khalsa* was founded in 1699 AD; Hazur Sahib

(Nander), the place where *Guru* Gobind Singh ascended to heaven. There are annual tours of *gurdwaras* organised by Sikh travel agents and many Sikh women take advantage of them. One fifty-year-old woman said that she and her husband receive a pension which makes them financially independent and that they would like to spend it on such tours. This would give them the company of other religiously-minded people and also a change of scene.

Sikh religious celebrations
Gurupurbs

Sikhs celebrate anniversaries of their *Gurus,* called *gurupurbs.* *Gurdwaras* celebrate *gurupurbs* elaborately, commemorating the births and deaths of the *Gurus* and important events in their lives. Some are celebrated more than others. The most important seem to be the martyrdom of *Guru* Arjun Dev (May or June), the birthday of *Guru* Nanak (November), the martyrdom of *Guru* Tegh Bahadur (November-December), and the birthday of *Guru* Gobind Singh (December-January). The *Namdhari sangat* celebrates *Hola* combined with the Birthday of *Satguru* Balak Singh and Pratap Singh. They also combine the celebration of *Basant Panchami* and the birthday of *Satguru* Ram Singh. The *Nishkam Sevak Jatha* celebrates some additional *gurupurbs*, such as *Guru-gaddi gurupurb*, which falls in September. The birthday of *Mata* Sahiban Devan, the wife of *Guru* Gobind Singh is celebrated in November by and for Sikh women. Children celebrate the martyrdom of the four *sahibjadas* (*Guru* Gobind Singh's sons) in December. The *Niskam Sevak Jatha* also celebrates the anniversaries of *Baba* Puran Singh in June and of his wife in February. The birthday of *Bhagat* Ravidas (a Hindu saint from a low caste) in February is also celebrated.

All the *gurupurb* ceremonies start with *Akhandpath*, which normally begins on Friday morning and finishes on Sunday morning. *Akhandpath* is the continuous recitation of the entire *Guru Granth Sahib* with *granthis* working in relays. It takes approximately forty-eight hours. On the first day of each lunar month, *Sangrand* is celebrated in *gurdwaras*. Many *gurdwaras* start *Sadharan path* (the ordinary recitation of *Guru Granth Sahib*) on this day and hold *bhog* (the finishing ceremony) on the next *Sangrand*. The *Nishkam Sevak Jatha* follow *Sampat path* in which they repeat and stress *gurbani* in order to reinforce their message, whereas *Namdharis* recite *varni da path* in times of distress, praying to God for his blessing. Women who can read the *Guru Granth Sahib* take part in *Akhandpath* and some women also participate in *kirtan*. Many women told me that it was an exciting time for them religiously and socially.

Sikh festivals

There are many popular Indian festivals, some of them are celebrated by Sikhs. However, the Sikh *Gurus* gave these an added religious interpretation. The most important Sikh festival is *Vaisakhi*, widely celebrated by Sikhs all over the world. It is the Spring harvest festival in India and particularly in the Punjab. Sikhs celebrate this day to mark the birth of *Khalsa Panth*, which gave them a distinct identity and code of conduct. Initiation ceremonies are widely held in *gurdwaras*. *Akhand Path* is performed and *langar* is served for all three days. There is also a *Nagar Kirtan*, a religious procession carried out by Sikh *sangat*, in which women are the main participants. *Diwali*, the festival of lights, is the most popular festival celebrated by Indians. On this day, Sikhs celebrate the release of their sixth *Guru* Hargobind, from Gwalior jail. On his release, he went to the the city of Amritsar where he was given a tumultuous welcome. One woman told me that Diwali in Amritsar was worth seeing. *Hola* is the day after the Spring Equinox, signifying victory over evils. *Hola* is a particularly significant festival for the *Namdhari sangat*. On this day, in 1680, *Guru* Gobind Singh decided to perform mock battles and military exercises in the presence of the Sikh community, stressing the desirability of strength along with the purification of their souls so that they were able to withstand evil. Since then *Hola* has been observed every year by holding processions displaying weaponry to indicate the importance of social discipline. Anandpur (a city in the Punjab) remains the principal location of this festival. *Gurdwaras* in England hold an evening *diwan* on the day. *Namdharis* celebrate *Basant Panchami* which is a festival marking the beginning of Spring season, but they celebrate it on a grand scale, making it more elaborate to commemorate the birthday of *Satguru* Ram Singh.

The festival of *Lohri* falls on *Makar Sangrand*, around mid-January. In the Punjab, it is celebrated in homes, but in England *gurdwaras* have a special *diwan* on this day. It is a common tradition among Sikhs to celebrate *Lohri* if a boy is born or a son gets married. I was told that Sikh women generally celebrate the first *Lohri* in the *gurdwara* rather than at home. *Maghi* also falls in January and is named after *Magh*, an Indian lunar month. It is normally celebrated in the *gurdwara* and not at home. It is connected with the battle of Mukatsar where *Guru* Gobind Singh found forty men from Majha who had deserted him during the siege of Anandpur. Their women-folk were so ashamed of them that they would not let them enter their homes. The men then returned to reinforce the *Guru*'s small army, and died fighting for him. The *Guru* was deeply moved and tore up the paper in front of *Bhai* Maha Singh on which they had written their *betaba* (disclaimer), as a sign of forgiveness and reconciliation. He embraced each one of them, as they lay dead or dying, and called them the 'Saved Ones'. This *mela* (festival) of *Maghi* is celebrated in their memory at Mukatsar and many Sikhs go there.

Sikh women seem to be knowledgeable about religious festivals and they fully participate in path, *kirtan* and *langar seva*. It was noted during the interviews that many young Sikh women did not understand the significance of *Hola* and *Maghi*. Some younger women said that they had discovered the importance of these festivals through the celebrations in *gurdwaras* and a few said that they had read about them in books and discussed them at school in their religious studies classes. Sikh religious books are also produced by the Sikh Missionary Society, which was founded in 1969 by a group of teachers in Gravesend. The society appreciated that the teachings on Sikhism in *gurdwaras* and by parents were insufficient, and that there was a pressing need to reinterpret Sikh traditions and to show young Sikhs how the *Guru*'s teachings could provide answers, even to questions asked by children in a British context. They have published some well-written books in English containing historical accounts of the *Gurus*' lives, moral teachings, and simple translations of important passages of *Gurbani*. One Sikh woman said that these English texts helped young people to understand the spirit of the Sikh religion, especially those aspects of the *Gurus*' teachings that were most relevant to the problems of living in a complex industrial society. One eighteen-year-old Sikh woman said that well-produced television documentaries were also very useful for the younger generation to understand different aspects of religion.

She mentioned a documentary produced by the BBC in 1999 on the tri-centenary celebration of *Vaisakhi*. Many women quoted the *Lashkara* channel as a useful source of religious information.

The normative beliefs of Sikhs and the way in which these are applied in practice by Sikh women in the Punjab and in England have been discussed here. In general, it appears that religion, or at least religious observance, continues to play a dominant part in the lives of Sikh women. They go to *gurdwaras* regularly. Their lives revolve around the *gurdwara* as all life cycle rites and religious festivals take place there. Although their adherence to religion is strong, it appears that they do not always seem to follow Sikh teachings and traditions in their entirety. The religious perception of some Sikh women suggests that they have faith in the spiritual tradition of Punjab reflecting their daily beliefs and practices which are far removed from the normative values.

Further Reading

Adi Granth. Amritsar: Shromani Gurdwara Prabandhak Committee. (Standard version of 1430 pages in Punjabi)

Cole, W. O. 'Sikhism'. In *A Handbook of Living Religions* ed. by J. Hinnells. Harmondsworth: Penguin, 1984.

Cole, W. O. and Sambhi, P. S. *The Sikhs: Their Religious Beliefs and Practices*. London: Routledge and Kegan Paul, 1978.

Drury, B. 'Sikh girls and the maintenance of an ethnic culture'. In *New Community*, 17 (3), 1991. 387-399.

Ghuman, P. 'Bhatra Sikhs in Cardiff: family and kinship organisation'. In *New Community*, 8 (3), 1980. 308-316.

Helweg, A.W. *Sikhs in England. 2nd edition*. Delhi: Oxford University Press, 1966.

Johar, S. S. *Handbook on Sikhism*. Delhi: Vivek Publishing Company, 1977.

Kohli, S. S. *Sikh Ethics*. New Delhi: Manoharlal, 1975.

Macauliffe, M. *The Sikh Religion*. New York: Chand, 1963.

McLeod, W. H. *Sikhism: Textual Sources for the Study of Sikhism*, edited and translated by W. H. McLeod. Chicago: University of Chicago Press, 1990.

Malcolm, J. (Sir). *Sketch of the Sikhs*. London: John Murray, 1812.

Sikh Rahit Maryada. Amritsar: Shromani Gurdwara Prabandhak Committee, 1992.

Singh, A. *Ethics of the Sikhs*. Patiala: Punjab University,1991.

Singh, G. (tr.) *Guru Granth Sahib*. Amritsar: Shromani Gurdwara Prabandhak Committee, 1984.

Singh, G. *A History of the Sikh People (1469-1978)*. New Delhi: World Sikh University Press, 1979.

Singh, J. *The Sikh Revolution: A Perspective View*. New Delhi: Bahri, 1981.

Singh, K. *The Sikhs*. Calcutta: Lustre Press, 1984.

Singh, P. *The Sikhs*. London: John Murray, 1999.

3

Women in Sikhism and Sikh Society

The status of women is clearly defined in Sikhism. Sikh teachings lay emphasis on all kinds of equality, placing a high value on human dignity. The Sikh *Gurus* emphasised gender equality in particular, giving full and equal status to women. The vision of the *Gurus* on this matter was far ahead of their time. The authoritative work on this subject is the *Guru Granth Sahib*, supported by the words and practices of the Sikh *Gurus* and the *Rahitnama* (Sikh Code of Conduct).

In the fifteenth century, at the time of the first Sikh *Guru, Guru* Nanak, two religions, Hinduism and Islam, were dominant. The position and status of women was influenced by Hindu and Islamic values, as interpreted by scholars and theologians of the time, and also by social values. The structure of Indian society was patriarchal (male head of family) and male supremacy was reinforced and perpetuated in the name of religion.

In general, the condition of women was humiliating. They were considered to be inferior and the property of their fathers, husbands and sons. Their function was only to perpetuate the race, to do housework and to serve the male members of their families. They were considered to be seducers and distractions from man's spiritual path. Men were allowed to practice polygamy (having more than one wife), but widows were not even allowed to remarry. In some parts of India, they were encouraged and sometimes even forced to commit *sati* (committing suicide by throwing themselves on to their dead husband's funeral pyre). Child marriage and female infanticide (the killing of girls at birth) were practised. *Purdah* (veiling) was common among women in north India. Women were rarely allowed to inherit property. They did not participate in public affairs but generally remained secluded in the home.

Sikh ideology and the status of women

The Sikh *Gurus* adopted a two-fold approach to gender issues. They assumed a positive attitude towards women in order to enhance their status and prestige. They condemned the social and religious practices then prevalent in Indian society, which undermined the status of women and they argued for women's liberation. *Guru* Nanak declared that women must be respected, as they were the source of humanity's physical existence and of its entire social structure.

> It is by woman, the 'condemned' one, that we are conceived and from her that we are born; it is with her that we are betrothed and married.
> It is the woman we befriend, it is she who keeps the race going
> When one woman dies, we seek another; it is with her that we become established in society.
>
> Why should we call her 'inferior', who giveth birth to great men?
> A woman is born of a woman; none is born without a woman.
> O Nanak, only the Lord has no need for a woman.
> [Asa di Var, *Mohalla*: 475]

In the *Guru Granth Sahib*, women are the bonds of life and the world and they unite the family. The woman receives great veneration in Sikh society as 'she gives birth to kings and divines' (*Adi Granth*: 473). As a mother, she receives the respect of the whole society and as a wife she is the better half of man. From this scriptural authority, it is clear that women are given a high position in Sikh society. *Guru* Nanak and the other *Gurus* allowed women an equal share in both social and religious life.

Sikh Religion and religious practices

The Sikh *Gurus* invited women to join the *sangat* (congregation) and work with men in preparing the *langar* (common kitchen). The tradition of *langar* in Sikhism goes back to *Guru* Nanak, but the third *Guru* emphasised this tradition as a device for expressing the theoretical notion of equality in a practical way (Cole and Sambhi, 1978: 22). *Guru* Amardas also introduced the concept of *pangat* (row), where all had to sit in a row and eat together irrespective of their caste and status. Sikhism allowed women full participation in religious activities. *Guru* Amardas appointed fifty-two women missionaries out of one hundred and forty-six to spread the Sikh message and, of twenty-two *Manjis* (dioceses) established by the *Guru* for the preaching of Sikhism, four were headed by women (K. Kaur, 1992: 99). *Bibi* Amro, daughter of *Guru* Angad, was one of them. The contribution of *patasha* (sugar crystal) in the preparation of *amrit* (baptismal water) by the wife of the tenth *Guru* was also an indication of the participation of women in religious activities. *Guru* Gobind Singh opened up the initiation ceremony to both men and women. Following the efforts of the Sikh *Gurus*, women could join and lead the holy congregations, take part in the recitation of the Holy Scripture, work as *granthis* and preachers.

Previously, the idea of *sannyasa* (abstaining from worldly comforts and pleasures) had influenced attitudes towards women in India. The inherent attraction of the female had been considered to be a temptation; something against which the *sannyasi* must be warned and to which he must not be attracted. The *Gurus*, however, did not regard women as hurdles or obstructions on the path to salvation. They rejected the idea of taking *sannyas* (asceticism or renunciation) and regarded family life, if it was led in a righteous manner, as superior to that of the ascetic (*Adi Granth*: 26). In order to emphasise the superiority of the householder's life, the Sikh *Gurus* placed great emphasis on marriage and family life and they advocated marriage between two equal partners. *Guru* Amar Das, the third *Guru*, wrote, 'Only they are truly wedded who have one spirit in two bodies (*Ek jyot duo murti*)' (Adi Granth: 788).

Marriage, rather than being a union of bodies, was held to be a union of souls, of minds, leading to love of one another's qualities and care for each other's well being. The marriage relationship as mere sexual gratification was also condemned. *Guru* Hargobind, the sixth *Guru*, said that a wife was the conscience of a man (*aurat iman hai*) and she should act as a check and restraint on his weaknesses.

The *Gurus* redefined the model of virtue as being marriage to one wife and taught that male and female alike should practice conjugal fidelity. The practice of having more than one wife would run counter to the spirit of equality between the sexes. Only monogamous marriage was believed to fit the institution of the family.

The *Gurus*, by bringing this type of vision to people, expected that women would be given honourable status in every segment of society. Thus, according to Sikh ideology, woman was declared not to be inferior to man and as having equal responsibility for her actions before God (*Adi Granth, Var Asa*, xix). Sikhism suggested the practical steps to be taken for the socio-religious equality of women with men.

Socio-religious traditions

Female infanticide was a common practice in medieval India. The main reasons for this were superstition, the expense of the dowry for daughters and the difficulty of finding suitable husbands. The *Gurus* denounced the practice and they also found solutions for its causes. Sikhism advocated discarding the dowry system. 'No dowry ought to be accepted from the bride's parents' (*Sikh Rahit Maryada*: 28, xii). On the contrary, social help should be offered to parents experiencing difficulty in finding a match for their daughter and also in arranging her marriage: It was further added that those indulging in female infanticide were to be excommunicated from Sikhism, and others having any social relations with them were deemed punishable (*Sikh Rahit Maryada*: 23, xi).

Sati means the immolation of a wife on her husband's funeral pyre. It was believed that such an action by a wife would expiate the sins of three generations and would obtain for her the posthumous title of *sati*, when she was considered to be a chaste and virtuous woman. This hope and encouragement was used to induce women to kill themselves, while there was no such requirement for a man on the death of his wife. The Sikh *Gurus* rejected this custom and *Guru* Amardas declared, '*Sati* is one who lives contented and embellishes herself with good conduct and cherishes the Lord ever and calls on Him' (*Adi Granth*: 787). The virtue of a woman lay in the role she played in the family and not in her death. The *Gurus* also allowed widows to remarry.

The custom of *purdah* (veiling) came to the Punjab with Islam. *Purdah* was a form of covering, which took different forms such as the *burkah* (body cover), the *chadar* (shawl) and the *jhund* (face covering). It was a custom strictly enforced upon women, as a protection against the lustful eyes of men. The *Gurus* did not accept *purdah*, and stated that women ought not to be veiled (*Sikh Rahit Maryada*: 21). *Guru* Amardas was the first to condemn *purdah*. He believed it was demeaning for women (Kohli,1975: 56). The immediate effect of the removal of *purdah* was that the spirits of women were raised by the belief that they were not helpless creatures, but were responsible for defending their own honour and dignity.

The status of women in Sikh society

The Sikh *Gurus* laid down the foundations of an egalitarian and progressive society. They advocated the principle of gender equality as the only true basis of good social relations. They promoted rights and privileges for women, both in religion and society. It is important, however, to evaluate the operative values of the Sikhs in order to judge the real position and status of Sikh women and also whether the teachings of the *Gurus* are followed in practice.

Today, Sikh women seem to have considerable freedom and equality in religious matters. They are allowed to participate in and lead the religious congregation. They have equal rights to initiation and worship. They take part in the continuous recitation of the *Guru Granth Sahib*. Women are fully involved in and contribute to the areas of *seva* (voluntary service) although they are under-represented in the management of *gurdwaras*. They cannot come forward and participate in management structures especially in areas of direct concern and relevance to women and children. Sikh women have more freedom than some other Asian women in terms of religious behaviour, but the *Gurus'* teachings of equality have never been fully realised in practice.

Female infanticide and *sati* were legally abolished in India in the nineteenth century. However, the custom of veiling and the preference for male children has remained with Sikh women even today as a legacy of Punjabi culture. The Sikh religion asserts that a child is a blessing from God, but the preference for a boy is common. Asian women, including Sikh women, are disposed towards sex pre-selection techniques that sometimes result in the abortion of female foetuses, giving a modern twist to female infanticide. The wearing of the veil, in spite of the *Gurus'* teachings and rejection, remains in place within traditional families of the Punjab, in the form of *ghungat* or *jhund* (face cover) and *chadar* or shawl (body cover). Sikh women do not practice *jhund* in this country. Child marriage was common among Sikhs in the first half of the twentieth century. As Sikh women's education increases, the age of marriage has risen and child marriage has become rare. Now, with more young women entering higher education, they are more likely to marry around the time they finish their first degree – around twenty-one or twenty-two or older. The current trend is towards later marriage.

Sikhs support the idea of widows remarrying and parents often insist that a young widow do so. There is also a growing tendency for divorced women to remarry. In the past, this was uncommon. Polygamy is rare within the Sikh community except in the case of 'barren' women.

It is still common to measure a woman's value as a bride by the size of her dowry and not necessarily by her character and integrity. Although there is no fixed system, the giving of a dowry persists within the Sikh community and is increasingly becoming a status symbol. This can create difficulties for parents on a low income and also leads to marriages being based on wealth instead of the suitability of partners.

Women normally have more than an equal say in domestic matters and matters concerning their children, but their participation in public matters is still limited. Whether it is the influence of the majority community on the Sikh minority, or the Sikh male's unwillingness to give up his dominant role, women continue to suffer prejudice. One of the reasons for their subjugation is the influence of Punjabi culture: women from rural backgrounds tend to be submissive and expect their daughters and daughters-in-law to behave similarly. There are a number of sayings within the Punjabi community which serve to uphold stereotypes of women, for instance, '*gut picche mat*' (women lack wisdom) and 'women are like an old coat or shoes and you can replace them when you want'. These sayings express a sense of male superiority which very much dominates Punjabi culture. Historically, the earning capacity of males contributed to their superiority, as women were generally housewives and not wage earners. Women as wage earners are now threatening traditional patriarchal structures. This has caused a reaction in the form of the re-emergence and support for ideologies that stress women's traditional roles. Alice Basarke has written that despite a head start of 500 years, Sikh women are no better off than their counterparts in any other religion or nation. In this country, Sikh women are combining paid work and domestic duties in the same way as do the women in the host community. Their external responsibilities have increased substantially, but they are still expected to carry out traditional roles of cooking and cleaning.

Many young Sikh women expressed their frustration and confusion at the hypocrisy in the Sikh community about the subjugation of women. Double standards operate in certain social situations; for example men may go out late at night and may date, whereas women experience social restrictions. Women are put under many social and cultural restraints and their movements are closely watched. Women are also discouraged from having any kind of interaction with the opposite sex. Even sitting next to brothers, cousins and uncles is often disapproved of. A woman should not look into a man's eyes, nor raise her head at her elders. She should never argue with her husband or his family. A woman should not defend herself even if she is right. Such restraints are expected only of women, not men. Inevitably they rob women of their strength and power and cramp their personality. *Laaj* (honour), *sharam* (shyness) and *izzat* (family prestige) are the words used for a woman's chastity, family prestige and honour. These are considered to be a woman's *shingar* (ornaments) and she should not lose them at any cost. Their actions can damage family *izzat* whilst men's actions are not considered damaging at all.

In spite of the exhortations of the Sikh *Gurus*, women remain less than equal to men in Sikh society. Although Sikh women are in a better position in some areas, real equality has not yet been achieved. Sikh women are enormously influenced by Punjabi culture and cannot distinguish between religious values and traditional social values of Punjabi culture. The main influences upon them derive from their parents, who were brought up and lived in an environment dominated by social rather than religious values. Sikh society like any other Asian society is male dominated and it is hard for some to treat women equally.

Further Reading

Basarke, A. *Where are the Women? Current Thoughts on Sikhism.* Chandigarh: Institute of Sikh Studies, 1996.

Cole, W. O. and Sambhi, P. S. *The Sikhs: Their Religious Beliefs and Practices.* London, Routledge and Kegan Paul, 1978.

Kaur, Kanwaljit. *Sikh Women: Fundamental Issues in Sikh Studies.* Chandigarh: Institute of Sikh Studies, 1992.

Kaur, Upinder Jit. *Sikh Religion and Economic Development.* New Delhi, National Book Organisation, 1990.

Kohli, Surinder Singh. *Sikh Ethics.* New Delhi: Munshilal Manoharlal, 1975.

Mandelbaum, D. G. *Society in India: Continuity and Change.* Berkeley: University of California Press, 1972.

Manu, *The Laws of Manu.* In Buhler, G. (tr.) *Sacred Books of the East*, xxv, ed. by Max Muller. London: Oxford University Press, 1886.

Millett, K. *Sexual Politics.* London: Rupert Hart-Davis, 1969.

Midgeley, M. and Hughes, J. *Women's Choices, Philosophical Problems Facing Feminism.* London: Weidenfeld and Nicolson, 1983.

Sharma, A. *Sati: Historical and Phenomenological Essay.* Delhi: Motilal Banarsidass, 1988.

Sharma, A. *Today's Woman in World Religions.* Albany: State University of New York Press, 1993.

Young, K. K. Women in Hinduism. In Sharma, A. *Today's Woman in World Religion.* Albany: State University of New York Press, 1993.

4

The Social Life of Sikh Women

The social life of any society is based on the way society thinks and conducts its life. Social life includes education, occupation, life style and social activities that enhance the quality of life. It is also shaped by its resources, work ethos and social activities which are linked to the traditions and values of that community. The social life of Sikh women is illustrated here by findings of the sample survey, which revealed that they are brave, hard-working and face many challenges in order to make their lives successful. They have a strong desire to achieve and enhance family prestige. They take life as it comes, believing in *bhana manana* (the will of God). They work very hard but at the same time know how to enjoy life. Sikh women are admired because of their generosity and hospitality. This chapter looks at the occupations of Sikh women, their attitude towards education, their aspirations and their lifestyle. Although the roots of Sikh women are in the Punjab, their backgrounds differ widely. The Sikh community may give the impression of being a homogeneous group, but the diversity created by the various religious sects and castes influences their social life.

The occupations of Sikh women
Traditionally, Sikh women in rural Punjab did not work outside the home for a salary. A small proportion of educated urban Sikh women from India and East Africa worked mainly in teaching, medical-related professions or as administrative clerks in offices

and banks. Two of my sample had worked in India (one as a teacher and the other as a school librarian) and three had worked in East Africa (in teaching and administration). Rural women worked with their fathers or husbands, depending upon the family occupation. Examples included working in the fields, weaving and as domestic servants. Sikh women of high status in the Punjab did not work.

Coming to England changed that pattern. Those who came here from India could bring only £3, all that was legally allowed. The men who had settled in Britain before their wives sent substantial amounts of their earnings 'back home' and had hardly any savings. Friends and acquaintances used to pool their money to bring their families over. One early migrant told me that it took twelve years for her husband to bring his family here, as he could not raise the airfare. One fifty-eight-year-old Sikh woman told me that her husband's family asked him to send all the savings he had, which he did, and then he went to India to marry her. His family did not buy them a ticket for the return journey, which they had promised to do. Instead, they kept all the money and gave her husband a bill of marriage expenses, so he had to borrow money to return to England. Their first priority was to return the borrowed money and then to buy a house. This was the general pattern for Sikh families arriving in this country. The demand for money from back home was constant, despite the need for money to survive here. Sikhs sent as much as they could afford back to India in order to fulfil family obligations. When early male migrants lived on their own, they managed on the bare minimum by sharing rented accommodation and cooking communally. Their expenses increased as their families joined them and they had to have a house to accommodate their families.

Sikh women realised soon after their arrival that they could find work outside the home and contribute to the family income. At first, women from India struggled to get employment, especially when they could not speak English and were unfamiliar with the host culture. Slowly and gradually, they made their way into the labour market. I interviewed three Sikh women who came in the 1950s and they had all worked outside the home. One seventy-two-year-old who came in 1949, told me that she had stayed at home initially after having her children and then worked in a box factory for five years. She found it difficult to raise her family and work outside the home, so she opened a shop selling material for Asian women. She was the first woman in Leeds to have her own successful business, despite being illiterate and innumerate. She had no formal education and could speak scarcely any English. Another early migrant, now deceased, helped her husband with door-to-door selling. Eventually they ran their own warehouse and became fairly wealthy. Another seventy-year-old early migrant told me that she had stayed at home to look after her four children and sewed suits for women, as her husband had died soon after she joined him. She was educated and had an urban background but did not want to work outside the home and leave her children on their own. After a while, she was encouraged by a family friend to open a shop. She opened a fabric shop and combined her home sewing work with working there. Other early migrant women also opted for home-based businesses in order to combine work and home. They learnt that they could make more money running their own businesses than by taking jobs in factories. The other advantage was that by working from home they could avoid going out in cold weather. Neither did they risk embarrassment because of language and cultural barriers. Sometimes women helped their husbands at first with door-to-door selling and later with stalls in the local market. Some female entrepreneurs opened their own fabric shops in their homes. They were fairly successful, considering their rural background, literacy level, language and cultural barriers and the absence of support from the extended family.

In the 1960s the majority of Sikh women arriving from India had little or no education and were engaged in low-paid menial jobs in factories, undertaking sewing, pressing, packing and light engineering work. The pattern was that one woman would get a job and then would recommend other friends for jobs. I was told that plenty of work was available in the 1960s. Sikh women who came from India were able to get and hold on to their jobs, in spite of language and cultural barriers. Some women worked in factories during the week and helped their husbands in their businesses at weekends and in the evening. One informant said that employers were happy with Sikh women since they were not only hard working but reliable, as they hardly took any time off. Sikh women gained their employers' confidence and trust, which helped in creating later opportunities for East African Sikh women. Sikh women were unaware of their employment rights and their only concern was to earn money to meet their increased family expenses and buy their own houses. By the mid 1960s, most Sikh women worked unless they had young families and did not want to leave their children with child-minders. A few educated Sikh women from India tried to top up their qualifications, whilst others were happy to work in factories. In factories, these women played the role of intermediary between the employer and other Sikh women employees, overcoming language barriers. Later, some were able to get clerical jobs, as and when opportunities occurred. A few professional women tried to re-enter their professions, starting at the bottom of the ladder, but some educated women were content with factory work, thinking that these jobs were better paid than clerical ones.

It was also relatively easy for the older East African Sikh women to get jobs when they came to England in the late 1960s. They made their way into the employment market through their friends and acquaintances already working in British factories. Most of them were uneducated and could hardly speak English. They did the same jobs in factories as other Sikh women did. Some families with a business background in Africa opened their own businesses involving other family members. There seems to have been little unemployment in Sikh families, despite external racial discrimination and poor economic climates at times. Young Sikhs have been able to find employment within the system of small shops and businesses owned and run by Indians.

The young educated East African born Sikh women tended to get office jobs. They had their families before adding to their qualifications and then progressing in their careers. The situation has been very different for British-born and educated Sikh women. In the 1960s and 1970s Sikh girls went to school but rarely on to higher education. Many girls looked for a job after completing their schooling, but did not want to do the jobs their mothers had done. They sought office jobs and worked for two or three years on low pay, to save for their dowry. They were married young and few had the opportunity of higher education. Most of the Sikh women who are now in their thirties and forties were married before they were twenty. One thirty-seven-year-old woman told me that she was married at eighteen, had a number of low paid jobs and had two children. She started studying as a mature student when her children grew up. She now has a well-paid, full-time job. Many career women followed this pattern. It is to their credit that they had their families, looked after their children, combined education and work and are now in full-time employment furthering their careers.

Although Sikh parents take pride in educating their children, when they first arrived in England they were keen to marry their daughters young to prevent any chance of their becoming independent. Young Sikh women were kept under strict supervision and control until they married, whereas nowadays they are increasingly moving into higher education, attending university and studying for professional qualifications. They are entering professional jobs and are career-minded. I found Sikh women in my survey who are teachers, nurses, lawyers, accountants, beauticians, opticians, chemists, doctors, artists and writers. However, within the local authority only a few Sikh women are in senior positions and most work in low grades. Although more women are career-minded, Sikh parents are still very protective of their daughters. They are not against education but firmly believe that higher education makes girls too independent. They believe that allowing girls more freedom can risk family *izzat* (honour). They do not wish to restrict their daughters' education but disapprove of sending them away from home to study and are still keen for daughters to marry before they are twenty-five. In spite of this attitude, some Sikh women do go away to study and two of the women in this survey were working away from home in London. It appears that education has made many young Sikh women independent and assertive. They have become more westernised in their outlook and tend to make decisions for themselves – which only confirms their parents' concerns.

The majority of Sikh women combine work and family in a successful and balanced way. Even if wage earners, they still have the responsibility of maintaining the household in addition to furthering their career. The survey appeared to show that caste and status, even though important to the Sikh community, played no part in women's choice of occupation. Occupations followed by Sikh women are based purely on what work is available.

Housing

The early migrants from India lived in rented accommodation until they could afford to buy their own houses. Initially, Sikhs

lived in poor and crowded living conditions and restricted re-
creational facilities. Sikh women worked long hours (including
weekends) in factories in order to save money to buy a house.
Since then, patterns of living have changed immensely. Young
Sikhs prefer to buy houses in the suburbs, some distance away
from other Sikhs. Their attitude and way of thinking is quite different from that of first-generation migrants. Many Sikh families
own more than one house and one Sikh woman told me that her
family owned forty houses. Another said that it was easy for the
younger generation to move up the social scale. Her two children, aged twenty-six and thirty, own three properties each. She
observed that they have not had the family responsibilities that
early migrants had. They do not have to send money to family in
India or to support parents or relatives in this country. Their
attitude and way of thinking is very different from that of first-
generation migrants who had to struggle to buy a house and
settle.

The first priority of the earlier Sikh migrants was to buy a house
as soon as they could raise the deposit. This was partly because
of family need and partly because owning a house is a status
symbol within the Sikh community. They tended to buy big
through-terraced houses and would keep lodgers to pay their
mortgage who were friends, relations or people from their
villages. One early migrant told me that she and her husband had
bought a three-bedroom house, which was shared by three
families related to her husband. Another woman told me that
younger Sikhs find it strange that their parents used to live in
shared accommodation with their relatives, friends and distant
relations. Once a family of lodgers could afford it, they would
move out and buy the house next door or one in the same street.
Migrants from India normally bought their houses near each
other so as to feel secure and have easy access to each other, as
they felt lonely and isolated because of language and cultural
barriers.

The pattern of buying houses near each other changed with the
arrival of the East African Sikhs. Most came with capital and invested it in the property market. Some of them bought semi-detached houses in the suburbs and affluent areas and others
bought near their acquaintances, friends and relations. Some rich
business families live in large houses in affluent areas, built

according to their specifications. Other less well-off families, elderly couples and single mothers live in through-terraced houses and cannot commit to high mortgage payments because of their low income. Take-up of council flats and houses is generally negligible. In my survey conducted in Leeds, only two single women lived in council flats, and they did not seem to have any supportive family in this country. Elderly parents live with their sons if they do not own their own property. Some are happy to share accommodation with their sons and daughter-in-laws, whereas others have reservations. One elderly woman told me that she was unhappy living with her daughter-in-law but did not want to apply for a council flat, simply because this would damage family prestige. Another disclosed that she had a spacious, four-bedroom terraced house but her son had still bought his own house, leaving her alone.

Living standards
The living standards of the Sikh community have improved steadily from the rented, run-down homes with few facilities of the 1950s to the centrally heated, carpeted and furnished semi or detached houses of today. At first they shared accommodation until they could afford to buy their own properties, mainly back-to-back or through-terraced houses. In Leeds, most Sikhs now own large detached or semi-detached houses. The furnishing is modern and varies in style and quality depending upon taste and resources, although the style usually has an eastern flavour. Almost all Sikh families have hot running water as well as inside toilet and bath. Most Sikh householders have cars and many women have the use of a car.

Thus the lifestyle of Sikh women has changed greatly. One informant who was an early migrant told me, 'There was no bath in my house. We used to go to the public baths to have a bath and do our laundry. We used to heat water through the open fire back boiler. The house would only warm up if we put coal on the fire to burn. There were no carpets but old lino, which I used to scrub clean. Our life is cosy and luxurious now; carpets in every room, constant hot water, toilets, shower and bath inside, central heating, comfortable furniture and beds'. A sixty-five-year-old woman said, 'In the early days, no one bought new furniture and carpets. We used to buy second-hand furniture and lino. We could not afford to buy anything new.' A sixty-year-old Sikh woman told me that her husband bought a new wool carpet and furniture for their drawing room and his relations criticised him for wasting his hard-earned money. Another woman said that nobody had a fridge, dishwasher, or washing machine in those days. Younger Sikhs are able to buy new carpets, furniture and other household goods. Their living standard is far superior to that of their parents.

Lifestyle

Lifestyle covers many things, such as food and its availability, dress, dress sense and the influence of the host community over such matters. Much more could be included under this heading but in light of the scope of this book the emphasis is on food and dress, which are of interest to all Sikh women.

Food

The Sikh staple food is wheat and the Sikh diet consists mainly of wheat flour, butter, *ghee* (clarified butter), milk, milk preparations, spices, green vegetables, nuts and dried fruit. Sikh meals generally include *chapatis*, (flat bread) made of wheat flour, *sabzi* (vegetarian curry), *dal* (cooked pulses) yogurt or a preparation of yogurt and salad. Pulses and vegetables which are normally made into curries form the major part of the Sikh diet. Salads are served with fresh lemon juice. Sweet dishes and rice are prepared on special occasions and for celebrations but are not normally a part of the main meal. Chutneys and pickles may accompany meals. Non-vegetarian Sikhs eat meat and fish (curried or *tandoori*) but normally avoid eating beef out of consideration for the feelings of Hindus, with whom they share many values. Similarly they would avoid eating pork when they are in the company of Muslims. However, there is no religious prohibition about eating beef and pork.

The Sikh religion is not prescriptive about diet, suggesting that one eat what is suited to one's body. But Sikhs are divided over the matter of eating meat. The *Adi Granth* contains a number of verses, which can be read as a rejection or acceptance of the belief that eating flesh is polluting and should be avoided. 'Fools fight over meat. Man is born from flesh, his *atman* (spirit) lives in flesh. When he is taken from the womb of the flesh he takes a mouth-

Punjabi meals and snacks

ful of milk from teats of flesh' (*Adi Granth*: 1289-1290). According to the *Rahit Maryada*, Sikhs should not eat *halal* meat (from animals killed by the process of gradual slaughter). Meat is only permitted for consumption if it is *jhatka*, where the animal is killed instantaneously with one blow, though the survey reveals that Sikh families do not always adhere to that ruling. Sikh vegetarians see this as the rejection of a particular method of slaughter, not permission to eat meat killed in some other way. However, those who do eat meat consider that the prohibition permits the eating of meat killed at a stroke and not bled to death. Here the position of the Sikh teaching is far from clear. Many Sikhs will not eat any form of meat, rejecting fish as well as eggs, but for some the cow is the only forbidden animal and so they will not eat beef.

According to the survey, some Sikh women eat meat and often do not discriminate between *halal* and *jhatka*. Sikh families who eat meat may use halal meat and buy it from Muslim shops; others buy their meat from supermarkets. There is hardly any demand for *jhatka* meat by Sikhs so there are few *jhatka* shops and *jhatka* meat is not served at functions organised by local authorities, however many Sikhs attend. Most 'Indian' restaurants use *halal* meat. It is difficult to say whether the sparse use of *jhatka* meat is due to ignorance or unavailability. When I asked one woman the reason for eating *halal* meat, she replied that it was cheap.

Many Sikh women are vegetarians, because they believe that meat is prohibited in the Sikh religion. Certain Sikh-related sects like the *Namdharis* and *Niskam Sevak Jatha* are pure vegetarians and believe that meat and fish produce passion and lust. *Bhatras* and *Nirankaris* eat meat, and *Bhatras* even cook meat in their *gurdwaras*. Explaining the cooking of meat, one *Bhatra* manager said that *gurdwaras* in this country are not only religious places but also for social gatherings. This survey found that *langar* is always vegetarian and meat is never served, so that no visitor is embarrassed.

Sikh women believe in cooking with love and care. They observe cleanliness in preparing their food. They always wash their hands before touching food. They will not make the food *jhutha* (eating or tasting the food with the same spoon and then giving it to someone else) and *jhutha* food is not served to anyone. One informant told me that she could not even eat the left-over food of her own child.

The ingredients needed for the preparation of Sikh meals are easily available these days. One informant who enjoyed cooking told me, 'almost everything is available now. You name it and it is there'. A number of grocery shops and supermarkets sell ingredients at competitive prices. Open markets sell many vegetables used in Sikh cooking such as aubergines, peppers, *moolies* (a long white radish), mushrooms, garlic and ginger. Even exotic fruits like mangos, *rashbhari* (raspberry) and *luquart* are available. Another informant told me, 'preparing Sikh meals is no problem now. You can also prepare very sophisticated recipes with easily available ingredients'.

The early migrants told me that such ingredients were not readily available in the 1950s but could only be obtained in small quantities from a shop in London or if someone brought them from India. One informant told me how they would go to market and see what they could cook in an Indian way, from the range of vegetables available. They invented some new combinations and ways of cooking dishes. *Saag* (a kind of cooked mixed vegetable puree made mainly from green mustard), a popular and authentic dish, found new variations with green vegetables such as spring cabbage, spinach and sprouts. Another Sikh woman told me that Indian vegetables were very expensive when she came to England in 1968. She wanted to make *koftas* with gram flour, spices and *ghiya* (courgettes) but she could not afford to buy *ghiya* at 99 pence a pound, so experimented with marrow, which cost a few pence from the market. Sikh women in earlier days were always on the look-out for shops where they could buy even a limited range of suitable goods. One informant said, 'we could get lentils, *mooth* (a kind of pulse), dried peas and sometimes *bhindi* (okra) in one Polish shop'. Another told me that in 1962, an Asian shop opened in her town, soon followed by another Gujarati shop. They sold some spices and a few Indian vegetables. 'But there was not enough variety. Gradually the number of shops increased and ingredients became widely available and their variety increased.' These days almost everything is available as shops import tropical vegetables and other produce. There are Indian sweet shops in every big town and big supermarkets sell authentic Indian food such as *samosas, onion bhaji, chicken tikka* and many more dishes. As one woman commented, 'There is now more variety here than in the Punjab'.

The variety in cooked Indian food increased with the arrival of East African Asians. They had left India long before and had learned from each other how to cook sweets and savouries. Some professional cooks had had sweet shops in Africa, and they followed the same profession when they came to England. In almost all the towns in England with significant Sikh populations, women with a knowledge of cooking for large numbers run catering businesses from home. But few restaurants are run by Sikh women.

Enjoying variety, Sikh women began to include British ingredients and spices in their cooking. They modified English and continental recipes to suit Punjabi tastes. In many Sikh homes, pizza, noodles, cakes, pancake and various vegetable and meat preparations are found which have been modified from the original recipes. For example, pizza made in the Sikh home may be topped with onions, chillies and small pieces of mango. Women make mango mousse. They have adapted to British ways of cooking Sikh dishes, such as roasting chicken with Indian spices and steaming fish with garlic and ginger.

Many Sikhs still eat traditional meals and curries. Sikhs often categorise food into 'hot' and 'cold' – not in temperature but in effect. Foods that are salty and high in animal protein are generally considered 'hot' while foods that are sweet, bitter, sour or astringent in flavour are 'cold'. The Sikh diet is rich, containing milk, milk products, pulses, meat, fish and vegetables. It tends to lack iron, Vitamin D, Vitamin B12 and Folic acid, as I learned from a dietician.

The social separation of men and women has no place in Sikhism, but there is a cultural tradition in the Punjab for men and women to eat and socialise separately and in many Sikh homes men and women eat separately. Women feed their menfolk first. One Sikh woman said that it was thought respectful to give the first *chapati* to the head of the family. Generally males are fed before females can sit and eat, but Sikh families who are influenced by Western culture sit and eat together. I was told that in Britain it depended very much on the individual family as to whether they liked to eat together or separately.

Fasting

Fasting is fairly common among Sikh women, for religious and social reasons. Some women fast because they believe, as the Hindu religion suggests, that by fasting their desires will be fulfilled. Others fast for health reasons. They fast at intervals according to the calendar, particularly at the time of *astami* (the eight days in the bright fortnight of the Indian luni-solar calendar), *ekadashi* (the eleventh day in the bright fortnight) and *puranmashi* (full moon). A great majority of unmarried women fast on Mondays in order to secure a good husband, and married women fast for the general welfare of their husbands. Many women do not know that fasting is not sanctioned within Sikhism. Fasting simply as a religious observance was condemned by the *Gurus* as pointless and likely to lead to the sin of pride. In *Dhanasari Mahalla* 5 it is said, 'Neither worship (of gods), nor fasting, nor a saffron mark, nor ablution, nor (customary) charity, only contemplating the Lord's Name, one's mind is at peace' (*Adi Granth*: 674). Despite this condemnation, it was noted during this survey that *karva chauth*, a fast kept to secure the long life of husbands, was popular among Sikh women. Some women also observe other fasts on different days of the week and on different occasions for Hindu gods and goddesses, for instance, *Shiv ji da vart* (fasting for the blessing of Lord Shiva, a Hindu god). I asked some women their reasons for fasting and they replied that they have fasted from a young age and saw no reason to stop now.

Hospitality

Sikh women regard hospitality as part of their religious duty. Sharing food also has religious connotations. Sikh women told me that a guest, even if unexpected, received every attention. Food is offered to guests and no effort is spared to make them comfortable. Offering hospitality is thought to bring great credit and blessings to the host. Sikh women are very generous in their hospitality. I was offered food and drink everywhere I went. Sikh women told me that it was important to share food as you never know whether God may be visiting you in disguise. They also said that those who were not hospitable would not have *barkat* (prosperity) in their homes. Generosity is a Sikh characteristic. Individuals see this as a matter of pride and contribute substantial sums to humanitarian causes, such as to sufferers of natural disasters. It is noticeable in the *gurdwaras* that Sikh women, especially older women, are at the forefront of contributions.

Dress

The Sikh religion does not prescribe any specific dress as long as the body is covered modestly and gracefully. Ancient dress for Sikh women was *kurti* (top), *salwar* (loose trousers) or *ryeb pyjama* (tight fitting trousers). Dress changes from time to time with the advent of new material and fashions. Punjabi folk songs reflect social life in the Punjab and many folk songs reflect the changes in dress (Sharma, 1988). One woman mentioned such a folk song, '*Nand Kaur sap ban gayi reb pyjama pa ke*', which means that Nand Kaur (the name of a woman) looks like a snake because she wears tight *pyjama* (emphasising the beauty of her flexible and slim figure). The Islamic influence encouraged women to wear *ghagra* (a heavy pleated long skirt) over the *salwar* and a large *chaddar* (shawl). I was told that almost all early migrant Sikh women had worn *ghagras* (long skirt) in the Punjab. The *ghagras* were made of black *souff* (cotton satin). One woman laughed and sang this song to me, '*Tera ghagra ras na ave suhreyan da pind agaya*' (you can not handle your *ghagra* (long skirt) properly, the village of your parents' in-laws has come near). From time to time, different cuts appeared, making the clothes tighter or looser as fashion dictated. Material used in India included *khadar* (coarse cotton), *lattha* (stiff cotton), crepe, linen, *sheint* (printed cotton) and silk. With the advent of manmade fibres, polyester became popular. Women sewed their own clothes by hand and later with sewing machines. Expensive clothes or clothes for special occasions such as weddings, were stitched by tailors. Fashion and styles changed often. At present there is immense variety in the fabric, embroidery and design used in the making of Punjabi suits, which have become popular. Ready-made suits are easily available and it is no longer necessary to sew clothes at home.

Sikh women normally dress in a Punjabi suit consisting of *salwar*, *kameez* and *dupatta*. A Punjabi suit could be made from cotton, man-made fibre (polyester), wool or silk. It takes 4-6 metres of material, depending on the size and design. A *kameez*, is a type of shirt normally 1.14 metres long, either tight or loose fitting. Women create designs on the neck openings (*galah*) by cut and embroidery. *Salwar* are loose fitting trousers, requiring 2.5 metres of cloth. A *dupatta* or *chunni* is a like scarf or shawl and is 2.25 metres long and 1.25 metres wide. It can be of net, cotton, chiffon, silk or man-made fibre and can be plain, printed or embroidered. The *saree*, even though it is the national dress of India, is not popular with Sikh women and is worn mainly by educated and urban Sikh women. The *saree* is worn with a blouse which covers the midriff and has a petticoat underneath.

Even after four decades in this country, Sikh women still wear basically the same dress, generally *salwar kameez*, even though there is no religious reason to do so. The Punjabi suit is the socially accepted dress for Sikh women. Around their shoulders or over their heads women wear their *dupatta*. Older women always cover their heads with it, whereas younger Sikh women tend to put it around their shoulders. Most women cover their heads in front of their elders in order to show them respect.

Punjabi suits come in a variety of styles and fabrics. Materials are available in a number of shops which also sell locally made and imported suits from Japan, India, Pakistan and elsewhere. Boutiques sell ready made suits at competitive prices and the quality and range varies enormously. Women also copy designs from fashion magazines and Asian programmes and have them made to measure. One informant told me that she had to pay £15-£25, depending upon the design, to have a suit made. I found that more and more women were having their suits made, even though they could sew. One woman told me that in the 1950s there was no specific material available in British stores to make Punjabi suits. She said, 'We used to buy net *dupattas* from one Muslim shop in the market and satin from a *gora*'s (white

Punjabi suit   *Saree*   *Lehnga suit*

person) shop and sewed the suits ourselves. Later in 1963 or 1964, an Indian woman opened a shop and we bought material from her but the variety was limited.' Gradually more shops opened and the range and quality improved due to competition. Many fabric shops, especially in London, Birmingham and Leicester, now sell suit and *saree* material.

Punjabi suits vary in design, for example, frock and *ghutva pyjama* (pleated frock and tight-legged trousers), *sharara* suit (short shirt and wide-legged trousers), *ghagra choli* (pleated long skirt and short blouse) and *lehnga* suit (long pleated skirt and top). Material can be purchased for as little as £1 a metre, which means a suit would cost about £10. At the other end of the scale, some fabric costs £30 per metre, and some women may spend over £500 on a ready-made embroidered silk suit. First generation Sikh women wear a Punjabi suit at home, at work and for social occasions, whereas young Sikhs wear them mainly at *gurdwaras* and on other social occasions. Modern Sikh women and some middle-aged, educated women

Bridal dress

wear a *saree*, which is considered elegant. One woman remarked, 'the suit is good when you have a slim figure but the *saree* is fantastic to cover bulges and a middle-age spread. I wear *saree* only, as it looks elegant and graceful'. British-born Sikh girls normally wear western clothes. I asked one young Sikh woman why and she replied that she felt easy in them and did not stand out at work. But they will wear a Punjabi suit or a *saree* at weddings, social functions and parties. They wear particular clothes on special occasions such as marriage, evening events and funerals. Sikh women also select their clothes according to their age; light colours in old age and bright colours for the young.

It was found in the survey that Sikh women were fond of all sorts of jewellery. Gold jewellery seemed to be the most popular choice among Sikh women. Every woman I interviewed wore gold jewellery such as chains, earrings, bangles and rings. It is a matter of prestige for Sikh women to acquire plenty of gold. One middle-aged woman told me, 'I do not normally wear gold as I have a senior position and also belong to a family where a simple life and education are more important than gold. However, I bought some gold as women often used to comment that I was so poor that I could not afford to buy any gold. I now wear this gold on social occasions'. Rich Sikh women also wear diamonds and precious stones. One business woman showed me her ruby jewellery set bought from Burma and another professional woman showed off diamond studs and an expensive diamond ring bought from a local dealer.

Sikhs are not supposed to cut any hair on their body. However this survey found that it was common for young Sikh women to trim or cut their hair. Even girls from *keshdhari* families do so. It has also become common to have eyebrows shaped and facial hair removed. Young Sikh women also shave their legs and arms. When I asked them why they replied that it was fashionable and enhanced their appearance. They also pierce their ears and noses for jewellery.

Social functions and celebrations

As the Sikh community became established in England, their social life began to improve. Sikhs from India had brought their families to this country and bought houses. The remittances sent back home slowly reduced and the dream of returning home faded away. They started spending money locally, which began to improve their lifestyle. East African Sikhs arrived in family units and from the start made England their permanent home. This helped Sikhs to organise their family and social life and also contributed to the increase in social functions and celebrations. In the life of a Sikh, there are three domestic rites: the birth of a son, marriage and cremation, which are of great social and religious significance. Sikhs also celebrate festivals socially and in *gurdwaras*. With the passage of time, these celebrations have become grand and expensive.

Birth celebration

The birth of a child is considered to be a blessing from God. Celebrations begin with pregnancy. Among Sikhs from the *Khatri* and *Arora* castes, a ceremony called *ritan* or *goadbharayi* is performed in the eighth month of pregnancy. The pregnant woman receives a new set of clothing and sweets from her mother, and the women of the *biradari* assemble to dress her in the clothing, as well as to share the sweets. At the beginning of the ninth month, the parents of the pregnant woman take her home with them so that she can be cared for. This custom does not apply in England as the family set-up is different and the baby is often delivered in hospital. The in-laws are informed when the baby is born. On the birth of a son, sweets are sent with the news of the newborn child. If the baby is born at the in-laws' house, the parents of the woman will visit her, bringing *ghiyo* or *dabra* (a preparation of flour, semolina, *ghee*, *jaggery* and dried fruit) to help her to recover her strength, along with gifts and clothes for the new baby, clothes for their daughter and her mother-in-law, a shirt or turban for the father-in-law and son-in-law. After five or six weeks, the parents bring their daughter home to give her *suskara* (presents given by woman's parents at the birth of the first child). *Suskara* given on the birth of the first child is substantial. It includes five suits of clothing and gold jewellery, such as a necklace or earrings or complete set for the daughter, two suits for the mother-in-law, shirts or turbans for the men-folk, eleven suits and a bracelet or *kara* for the baby, bedding and utensils with sweets and money, normally £21.

Sikh women celebrate the birth of their sons by distributing *ladoos* (an Indian sweet). They may celebrate on a large scale by holding big parties in halls or having *langar* in the *gurdwaras*, especially on the birth of their first son. Distribution of *ladoos* is vital on the birth of a son. One woman told me that because she did not distribute *ladoos* on the birth of her son, as her husband believed in sex equality, she then became the talk of the town. The birth of a girl is not rejoiced over, in spite of the equality advocated by Sikh *Gurus*.

It is a common social custom to visit the new baby and give *sagan*, normally £5 or £10. Some women do not visit the family for thirteen or forty days after the birth of the child because of *sutak*. *Sutak* is a belief that the house, particularly the kitchen, is contaminated for thirteen days after the birth of a child. Sikh religious teachings do not approve of *sutak*, but in spite of religious condemnation, some traditional women still believe in it. One Sikh woman told me that her sister-in-law did not visit her when she had her first child simply because of *sutak*. Another woman commented that the Sikh community had not changed with time. *Sutak* might be relevant in a village environment because of lack of hygiene and infection, but this was hardly applicable in this country. She felt that traditional women would carry on observing redundant traditions to show others how important these are.

Birthday celebrations are common in this country and some Sikh parents celebrate the birthdays of their sons and daughters by having a party and inviting their family members and close friends. Some Sikh girls celebrate their 18th or 21st birthday by having an elaborate party. A hall is booked for such occasions and food and drinks are lavishly served. Live entertainment includes *bhangra* groups or folk singers. Parties also include the British traditions of a birthday cake and giving gifts.

Marriage celebrations

Marriage celebrations are becoming increasingly elaborate within the Sikh community and many women in the survey expressed anxiety at the escalating expense. The simple marriages of the 1960s have been replaced by more sophisticated events. Some Sikh weddings in rich families are ostentatious and the gifts presented and the many festivities are characteristic of the overt consumption patterns that have been emerging over the past decade. The celebrations are a mixture of traditional ceremonies, ceremonies brought from East Africa and ceremonies from Britain, such as registry office marriage, the cake-cutting ceremony and holding a reception. The earning capacity of women is one of the most important factors related to the escalation of the dowry system in Britain, and parental wealth accounts for the elaborate and ostentatious marriage rituals. They reflect the more established community. A mother of four daughters said that it might be all right for rich parents with one or two daughters but it was worrying for her with a moderate income. One informant told me that *daaj* (dowry) started around 1965, when East Africans came to this country and has gradually grown since then, in quality and quantity. Before this, weddings were simple and only nominal presents were given to the bride.

The focus in the 1960s and 1970s was on the wedding day itself and excluded all pre-nuptial celebrations. The whole marriage procedure was short and mainly performed in the Sikh temples. Gifts exchanged were restricted to presents given by family and close friends to the couple on the wedding day. Nowadays with growing facilities in the *gurdwaras* and the *gurdwaras* employing full-time *granthis* (priests), marriages take place according to *guru-maryada* (compulsory rituals in the presence of the *Guru Granth Sahib*) and follow a definite pattern, which applies to all Sikhs. The two obligatory rituals are the *karmai* (the engagement) and *viah* (the wedding ceremony). Other ceremonies such as *rockna* (reserving the groom), *chunni* (a scarf sent to the bride by her future mother-in-law before marriage), *shahai chithi* (a few weeks before the wedding, the bride's parents send a letter announcing the exact date of marriage), *mehndi* (henna), *goan* (singing night), *giddha* (folk dance) and *maiyan* (rubbing with a mixture of flour, turmeric and oil), are optional and more flexible ceremonies. Modern public ceremonies like dinner parties and receptions are normally held in halls and hotels. The traditional pre-nuptial ceremonies such as *maiyan* and *chaura* are held at home or in a hall depending on the size of the extended family. These traditional ceremonies are part of the social customs of the Punjab and are no part of Sikh religious traditions but have nonetheless been added to the wedding festivities.

During this survey, many of the Sikh women interviewed discussed the various ceremonies related to marriage and I personally witnessed some wedding ceremonies. These ceremonies need to be explained sequentially. The first ceremony is the *rockna*, when the bride's male kin literally 'reserve' the groom so that offers of brides from other families should not be considered by his family. It is very much a family affair, with the bride's family bringing sweets and dried fruit, and a nominal amount of money is given to the prospective bridegroom with a *sagan* of dried dates. The next ceremony is the engagement (*karmai*), which is performed close to or on the day of marriage, before the actual wedding ceremony. Cole and Sambhi state that a betrothal ceremony may precede marriage but is not essential and not religious (1978:115). On the occasion of betrothal, the bride's relations bring boxes of fruit (normally five, seven or eleven) and *thals* (trays) of sweets (normally five) for the groom's family, called *sagan*. They also bring a gold *kara* (bangle), a standard sum of £21-£51 and turbans for the groom and his male kin for *milni* (introducing). The bridegroom is given a dried date and a *ladoo* (an Indian sweet) to eat by the bride's father, who also gives money and gold to the bridegroom. This ceremony signifies that the bridegroom and his kin have firmly accepted the alliance. A reciprocal ceremony is performed for the bride called *chunni charauna* (the giving of a headscarf), when the mother-in-law sends a *saree* or a ready-made suit with a heavily embroidered *dupatta* (headscarf), a gold ornament called a *tikka* and some-times a gold jewellery set, *sagan* money (most *sagan* ceremonies carry odd numbers as this is considered lucky) along with fruit and sweets, confirming that the girl now belongs to them. Dinner parties for the extended family and friends follow these cere-monies. After the engagement, a registry office marriage takes place and there is always a dinner party at the groom's house to mark this occasion. Alternatively, there is an arrangement in the *gurdwaras* to register the marriage after the wedding.

A few weeks before the wedding, the bride's parents send *shahai chithi* to the bridegroom's parents. Two days before the marriage, the *maiyan* ceremony takes place, when a mixture of flour, tur-meric and oil is rubbed on to the bride and bridegroom. This is a cleansing process, which was significant in the past but now remains as a custom. In some families, this ceremony is repeated three times. The *mehndi* (henna) evening is the most important, when the bride's hands and feet are decorated with henna and there is singing and dancing followed by a lavish spread of food. It used to be an exclusively female event but has now become more or less mixed. On the day before the wedding, the *chaura*

Mehndi and bindi patterns

evening is held, when the bride's maternal uncles bring a set of red bangles with the bridal suit in which she will get married, gold earrings or a gold jewellery set and clothes for the bride's family. Food and drinks follow this, as most relatives are present on this occasion.

Finally, the Sikh marriage ritual called *viah* (marriage) takes place. This is the most expensive event of the marriage procedure. The day starts off with a reception receiving the bridegroom's wedding party (*barat*), followed by *milni* when the important male relatives of the bride and bridegroom are introduced with a turban and £5 given by the bride's father, and flower garlands are exchanged. The maternal and paternal uncles sometimes receive gold rings from the bride's father in the *milni* ceremony. The bridegroom's party and the invited guests from the bride's side have breakfast together, consisting of *samosas*, *bhajiya* and Indian sweets, with tea made the Indian way.

Then the most important ceremony of the marriage is conducted, called *lavan*. On completion of this ceremony, all the relations give *sagan* to the bride and bridegroom, generally £5 or £10 to each. Lunch is served to all the guests and the *barat* in the *gurdwara*, hall or hotel. After lunch, the close relatives of the bridegroom go to the bride's house for tea and the *doli* (departure) ceremony, when the bride is sent off to the bridegroom's home. The sum of *vaidaygi* is given on the occasion of the *doli* to the groom's father by the bride's father.

Finally, the bridegroom's parents hold a reception in a hall or hotel on the same night or the following evening. The wedding cake is cut at this party – a western tradition adopted by Sikhs. Groups specialising in Indian film and folk music are hired to provide live entertainment. The final ceremony in the marriage procedure is the *murva dola*, when the bridegroom's relations return to the bride's home for lunch the day after the wedding, along with the bride. Clothes are given to the bridegroom, his family and close kin.

Namdhari Sikhs perform neither *rockna* nor *thakan*, nor the engagement ceremonies. They choose a suitable match and ask for approval from their *guru* and the marriage is performed according to *vedi viah*. The departure of the bride (*doli*) takes place from the *gurdwara*. *Namdharis* are not allowed to give any dowry.

According to one woman I spoke to, the decision to seek a marriage may be influenced by a number of factors. Normally an older daughter marries before her younger sister or brother, and a younger sister marries before her older brother. An older brother whose father has died waits until his younger brothers and sisters have completed their education or training. She told me that this was strictly observed while the decision for a marriage rested with parents but that these traditions were changing.

Under normal circumstances, the marriage takes place in the bride's home town. As Sikh teachings emphasise the value of family life, few Sikhs remain unmarried. Sikh weddings can take place on any day of the week, or in any month of the year. One woman told me that Sikh weddings did not often take place in the Punjab during the lunar months of *Bhado* (July-August), *Kartik*, (October-November) and *Poh* (December-January). This was obviously a Hindu influence (being the months associated with a period of rest by the God Vishnu). Sikh teachings suggest that all the days of the week and all the dates of the month have the same value. Sikh *gurus* ridiculed astrology and other forms of divination. However, according to another informant, some Sikh families believe in the power of Brahmans, obtaining horoscopes for their children when they are born, which they consult especially when a marriage has to be arranged. Astrologers are also consulted about the most auspicious days for a wedding ceremony. In Britain weddings are normally held at weekends and on bank holidays for convenience.

Death

When someone dies, relatives and friends are informed and appropriate arrangements are made for the funeral. In this country, the funeral is arranged by funeral companies, but in India the funeral is arranged by the family of the deceased, on the day of death and before sunset if possible. This is not applicable in Britain as funerals must be booked and can take a week or more to arrange.

When a woman dies, it is customary to wash and dress her in clothes brought by her family before cremation. This Punjabi custom applies both in the Punjab and Britain. Where no close relative from the woman's side is living in the same country, other relations bring whatever is necessary. Her own family also bring all that is needed for washing such as soap, towels and oil and other items such as a comb and make-up, even if her husband survives her. The woman's own family also pay for the wood for cremation and in Britain they give some money towards the cost of the funeral as no wood is required for cremation. It is common to have *path bhog* after the funeral, which is normally *Sadharan path*, kept for the peace of the soul of the dead. If the head of a family has died there is a turban ceremony after the *bhog*. On this occasion, relatives bring turban lengths to his successor, who is normally the eldest son. His in-laws normally bring the turban tied by him in public. The tying of the turban signifies that the responsibility for the family is now his and he has become the head of the family. This is followed by a communal meal marking the normality of life.

It is a custom in the Punjab to feed *Brahmans* on the anniversaries of dead *pitrs* (ancestors) every year in the period of *shradhs* (which normally falls in September-October). However, this is a Hindu tradition and according to the Sikh religion, the performing of *shradhs* is forbidden (*Adi Granth*: 332). Many Sikh women in the survey nevertheless admitted to performing *shradhs*. One woman told me that she fed five pious Sikhs every year during the *shradh* period.

Social festivals

Festivals in the Punjab mark the unfolding of the seasons, agricultural cycles and religious observances and rites. Their dates are calculated according to the lunar calendar. A lunar year consists of twelve lunar months. A lunar month is based on the time it takes the moon to complete one series of its successive phases, that is to say approximately 29.5 solar days. Dropping or adding lunar months achieves the coordination between the lunar year of 354 and the solar year of 365 days. One full cycle of the lunar phase from full moon to full moon makes a lunar month. On the day of the full moon (*puranmasi*), a month comes to an end and on the following day (*sangrand*) the next month begins.

Sikhs celebrate many events which have both religious and social significance. The major summer festival is *Vaisakhi*, named after the second lunar month, *Vaisakh*. One *Jat* informant said that it was a harvest festival in India and was celebrated by farmers all over the Punjab. The fields would be full of crops, especially if the rains had fallen on time. *Vaisakhi* may be interpreted as a festival of renewal; the previous agricultural cycle has come to an end and a new one is about to begin. The festival is celebrated with folk dances (*Bhangra*) and singing. One piece of folklore (explained by another *Jat* informant) is especially applicable to this festival:

> *O, jatta ayee Vaisakhi*
> *Kanka di muk gaye rakhi*

This saying is addressed to farmers and it means that *Vaisakhi* has come and they no longer have to guard their wheat fields. A Sikh woman in a recent *Vaisakhi* radio programme mentioned that the festival had an added religious significance for Sikhs as it means the creation of *Khalsa Panth*. *Vaisakhi* is also treated as New Year's day by Sikhs, although the first lunar month is *Chet*. *Vaisakhi* normally falls on April 13th. The date is fixed, being based on a solar calendar, though once every thirty-six years it occurs on April 14th. New Year cards are sent to friends and relatives and *Bhangra* events are organised by younger Sikhs. One young Sikh woman said that so far 'I have never missed a *Vaisakhi* *Bhangra* gig'.

Diwali is another festival widely celebrated by Sikhs. It is essentially a Hindu festival though it has religious significance for Sikhs too. The principal ceremonial observance at home on the occasion of *Diwali* is the worship of the images of *Ganesh* and *Lakshmi*, the harbingers of good fortune and prosperity and each house is cleaned (the walls would be whitewashed in India) in anticipation of a visit by the god of prosperity and good fortune (*Lakshmi*). In India, people leave their doors open in the hope that the goddess *Lakshmi* will visit their homes. One Sikh woman commented, '*Diwali* in India is so different. Everyone enjoys the occasion, houses are cleaned, and new clothes and crockery are bought. Relatives and friends meet to exchange gifts. There is no fun here'. The commercial classes clear their old accounts and look to *Diwali* as the beginning of the new business year. This fusion of commercial and religious traditions makes *Diwali* a major social festival. Houses are decorated and lit with *deevas*, small wick lamps (oil lamps made of clay), candles and multi-coloured electric bulbs. Fireworks are displayed and enjoyed by all. Families have feasts and exchange sweets and presents. Some women said that they made their favourite dishes and sweets and shared them with their family and friends. Another woman said that *Diwali* cards were available now, which she sent to her friends.

Lohri and *Holi* are other popular festivals from the Punjab. *Holi* is seasonal in its significance and secular in its celebration. The festival marks the beginning of Spring and usually falls in the month of *Phagan* (February–March). There is a Hindu mytho-logical legend attached to this festival about *Prahlad* and *Holika*, signifying the triumph of good over evil. The practice of putting vermillion on the forehead was the original way of celebrating this occasion, which later changed into the sprinkling of dry colours and coloured water on one another. One Sikh student said, 'There is no fun about these festivals here. Back home we enjoy our day by sprinkling colours on each other, by having a feast and playing *antakshri* (a group singing game)'. However, another woman said that Hindu temples in this country cele-brated *Holi* with the sprinkling of colours.

The festival of *Lohri* falls on *Makar Sangrand*, generally 12, 13 or 14 January. It is a day for almsgiving and patching up quarrels. For Sikh families, *Lohri* is celebrated following the birth or a marriage of a son. A fire is lit and corn, peanuts and sesame sweets are eaten around it. Other foods eaten include rice pud-ding, *halwa*, cornmeal chapatis and mustard leaf *saag*. Most Sikh women know about this festival. One said that on her first *Lohri* after her wedding, her mother-in-law invited family and friends.

A fire was lit and there was singing and dancing. All ate *makki di roti* and *saag* (cornmeal *chapatis* and mustard *saag*). On their departure, guests were given peanuts and sesame sweets. The girls in the family were given gifts of clothing and money. In the Punjab, *Lohri* is celebrated at home but in the UK it is celebrated in *gurdwaras*.

Sikhs celebrate Christmas much as the host community does, seeing it more as a social occasion than a religious one. Christmas cards and presents are exchanged with relatives and friends (especially British friends). Sikh families, especially those with young children, have Christmas trees. I asked one woman the reason for celebrating Christmas on such a large scale and she replied that children born and brought up in this country knew Christmas better than *Diwali* and wanted to celebrate it. My observation is that Christmas has more or less replaced *Diwali* for young Sikhs in England.

Entertainment

The main sources of entertainment for Sikh women are visiting family and friends and inviting them for meals. They love to listen to devotional and folk music and participate in *Giddha* and *Bhangra* on social occasions. They are very fond of watching Asian channels on the TV. They also go to the pictures and in their spare time they knit, sew, embroider and occasionally read.

Folk dance

Sikh entertainment is normally limited to the performing arts such as folk dancing and music. Two folk dances are particularly popular with Sikh women: *Bhangra* and *Giddha*. *Bhangra* is the most popular Punjabi dance, known for its vigour and speed. It is a collective dance performed jointly by men and women. The participants, usually more than six, dress in loose colourful clothes, and stand in rows opposite each other. The dance is performed to the beat of the *dhole* (a large two-sided drum), which sets the tone and the speed of the dance.

Bhangra (Folk dance of Punjab)

Giddha (Punjabi folk-dance)

Remixed Western style, *Bhangra* music is becoming popular with British-born young Sikhs. *Giddha*, like *Bhangra*, is also an energetic and impressive Punjabi dance, performed exclusively by women. Women drum a *dholki* (a hollow wooden cylinder, which bulges out in the middle, with parchment on both sides) and sing *boliyan* and *geet* (folk songs) to the beat of a spoon. Many Sikh informants told me that no happy occasion was complete unless there was *giddha* and *geet*. One middle-aged woman said that when she was younger, women never danced in front of men but this had changed now. Women freely dance on the stage at marriages and other functions.

Music

Sikh women are fond of listening to devotional, folk and classical music, particularly devotional and folk. It is believed that devotional music has tremendous power over the heart and mind of devotees. It frees them from sorrow and depression and lends enormous peace of mind. *Gurus* have described music as a means of attaining spiritual joy and transcendental bliss. Sikh women in this survey mainly listened to music through radio and television stations such as *Lashkara* TV and Sunrise radio. Sikhs have a great musical tradition, beginning with *Guru Nanak*, who preached his message accompanied by music. The singing of hymns is called *kirtan*, which literally means singing the praise of God. *Kirtan* is divine music which should bring out clearly the purpose, scope and philosophical content of the hymns. A music teacher told me that many young Sikh children were learning *shabad kirtan*.

Lokgeet (folk songs) are extremely popular among middle-aged and elderly Sikh women. One Sikh radio presenter told me that when she broadcasts old *lokgeet* on the radio, the telephone does not stop ringing with compliments and requests for more songs. *Lokgeet* is the most important single source of entertainment in the Punjab. It is performed in various forms, from light singing to vigorous dancing. The folk music of the Punjab, like any other folk music, is a reflection of social and cultural traditions. It is an expression of emotions and feelings on different occasions such as marriage (*suhag*) and death (*vayen*) and also connected to the relationships between husband and wife, lovers, brother and sister, mother-in-law and daughter-in-law, and between brothers. In other words, it is a complete sketch of the way a society lives. No Sikh ceremony or function is complete without *lokgeet*. One Sikh informant said, 'I listen to folk songs when I am sad. They are so closely related to life that you forget yourself. I have bought many recorded tapes of folk music and my favourite songs are sung by Surinder Kaur and Prakash Kaur'.

Classical music is complex and difficult to understand. It is based on *ragas* and *talas*. The *ragas* divide the octave in hundreds of different ways, each suited to the expression of a particular mood, whereas the *tala* reconciles the varying pulses of a thousand different lines through a complex structure of rhythm. One Sikh woman said that she might listen to classical music, but to appreciate it properly one had to understand *ragas* and *talas*.

In the 1950s and 1960s there were few organised or well-established Indian musical groups in Britain but they came into existence as the Sikh community grew. Today a number of groups perform live, run by individuals interested in singing and dancing, while others are coordinated and financed by funding bodies. In addition, there are Sikh organisations which arrange social functions such as *Vaisakhi*, *Diwali* and New Year. Their main purpose is to provide a venue so that Sikh families and their children can meet and socialise in a safe environment. These organisations also collect money for charities and hospices. There are also institutions and organisations which not only provide music and dancing classes, but also encourage well-known and newly emerging artists to perform. The younger generation is becoming more aware of Indian music and dance.

Radio and TV channels

There are many radio and television programmes in Punjabi relayed in this country. The popular radio station called 'Sunrise', based in London, broadcasts Punjabi songs and *shabads* and is listened to in most Sikh homes. A number of television channels broadcast Indian programmes twenty-four hours a day. *Lashkara* is an exclusively Punjabi channel and Zee TV a Hindi channel which also shows some films in Punjabi, Gujarati and so on. Channel East has cooking programmes, dramas and English programmes; Music Asia broadcasts songs twenty-four hours a day; Soni has entertainment and mixed programmes and B4U is a music channel. Almost all Sikh families subscribe to these channels and they are a major source of entertainment and information for Sikhs. Most Sikh informants said they no longer feel lonely at home as there are so many television programmes to watch. One woman said that she listened to the radio while working in the kitchen. A young woman said that she had not known how to cook very well but could now cook many delicious dishes thanks to listening to cookery programmes. Sikhs also go to see Asian films at the cinema as Asian movies are shown in most cities in England. Young Sikh women enjoy both Indian and English movies.

Other sources

Sikhs are a sociable and hospitable community with a tradition of oral communication. They visit families and friends and invite them for meals. Young Sikhs enjoy eating out and going to parties. Some Sikh women walk, swim, go to yoga and to the gym, but little interest is shown in other sports. In the Punjab, Sikh women spend their free time in the company of other women in the villages. They undertake handicrafts such as spinning, *darri* and *khes* weaving, embroidery (*shade*, cross-stitch, *sindhi*, *phulkari* and stitching with mirrors), knitting, crochet, sewing and making small artifacts like hand fans, tapes and

Phulkari and hand embroidery of Punjab.

baskets. They learn these skills by copying and practice. These valuable skills are
dying out in England and the older
women feel that young Sikh women do
not seem to have either the interest or
the time. Knitting and sewing are the
main skills now used by women. I observed during the interviews
that women were sewing clothes, that embroidered and painted
pictures hang in their sitting rooms and that some wore hand-
knitted sweaters. When visiting places where women met in
groups, I found 90 per cent of the women knitting. Older educated Sikh women read books and periodicals mainly in Punjabi.
Younger Sikhs tend to read in English but reading is not a
particularly popular pastime.

Social norms and social problems

Sikh women are expected to observe certain social norms. The
most important are those regarding relationships and sexual be-

haviour, which form the basis for *izzat*. Living in this country and adopting the British way of life has also given rise to some new social problems for the Sikh community.

Relationships and sexual behaviour

The sexual behaviour of young Sikh women is strictly monitored. Premarital and extra-marital sexual relations are prohibited within the Sikh religion and Sikh females seldom engage in either. Women, when single, are expected to be chaste and, when married, to be faithful to their marriage vows. One reason for this chastity is that females are watched closely by their parents. Some young women were not allowed by their parents to be interviewed by me and in other cases mothers sat in on the whole interview. Going out is restricted, although some Sikh parents have relaxed their attitude, allowing their daughters to go out with work colleagues. Young Sikh women are strictly prohibited from dating men, especially those from outside their caste, religion and culture. Nonetheless the survey indicates that young women prefer to go on dates with prospective partners before getting married. One young woman said that although her parents were strict, they allowed her to go out once a week with her work colleagues but her father had warned her that she must not date anyone. Another woman said that it was not fair that Sikh boys were allowed to go out while women were restricted.

Middle-aged and older women always avoid looking straight into the eyes of men and their elders, out of respect, but the younger generation, educated and working in a western environment, seldom observes such rules. Conversing with men, even in a natural and innocent way, is disapproved of by the Sikh community and is seen as flirting.

Social problems

Sikh women seem to have been successful despite unfavourable circumstances. Several of the early migrant Sikh women have succeeded in business, in spite of language and cultural barriers, and women in their thirties and forties are excelling in their careers. Their interviews suggest that even though it can be a struggle, they manage to combine family, education and career. The women of fifty and above are trying to overcome their isolation problems by participating in *gurdwara* activities. Young women are reforming and modifying some of their Sikh values to generate a new Punjabi culture: a fusion of Sikh and contemporary British values. The Sikh community is currently passing through a transition period, in which they have to find solutions to situations that result from living and working in a British culture and environment. The most significant of these are caused by racism, discrimination, by isolation, being single mothers and as unmarried women, drinking and, to a lesser extent, smoking and taking drugs.

Racism and discrimination

Sikhs have a distinctive external identity. As with other minority groups, they often come up against racism and prejudices. Racism is experienced in the workplace, in education and on the streets and has become a part of Sikhs' daily life. The women who worked in factories in the 1950s and 1960s found that they were paid less than their white colleagues. One woman related her experience during the 1960s and showed me evidence that she was paid less than a white colleague doing exactly the same job. Women who worked in factories told me that they were not allowed to talk to each other in any language other than English. Another respondent said that they were watched to see how often they went to the toilet. They were expected to work harder than white women.

It was, and still is, common practice that supervisors and managers are white. One council worker of forty said that it was difficult to work under someone who could not understand your problems. In many public services provided for ethnic minorities, the staff who provide the service are from black groups, while the boss is white. One elderly woman said that it was normal practice for white bosses to take the credit for her work. She added that she thought they practiced a 'divide and rule' policy with black members of staff.

Racism is experienced both in and outside the workplace. A fifty-five-year-old woman said she felt unsafe in certain areas of the city. 'One Christmas evening, after work, I was going shopping with my husband in the car. A young white boy of nineteen kicked my husband's car. My husband stopped the car thinking that there might be something wrong with it. He got out and asked the boy what was the matter. He responded by kicking my husband on his forehead with his steel-toed boots saying 'Why is a black bastard driving the car?' We were shocked by his behaviour, especially around Christmas, and what was more shocking was that no white person would give evidence even after witnessing the whole situation.'

Another woman told me tearfully that once when her twelve-year-old son was playing in the street behind her garden, two white boys kicked him, cut his hair and beat him. Her son returned home, pale and shocked and told her about the incident. She called the police, and her son gave a very accurate description of his attackers. She received a reply from the police a week later regretting that they had not found the boys. They stated that it was not a racial incident. This happened in 1986.

One Sikh community worker said that Asians often complained that the police never arrived in time when they were informed of an incident. She described how once when she was returning home with her children after an evening out, three white boys jumped on the bonnet as she was taking her car into her driveway and shouted racial abuse. She locked her car from inside, found her door keys and told them politely to get off the bonnet, but they did not move. She got out of the car with her two children, ran into her house and rang the police. As soon as the boys heard her ringing the police, they ran away. She quickly went out and locked her car. The police arrived one and a half hours later. The woman got very angry and when she asked the reason for this delay, the policeman said that they had been unable to find the house. She remarked, 'This is the way the police 'protect' black people, thus losing their confidence. They can guess us from our accent'. Numerous other incidents were related by the women: of racial harassment at work, in schools and playgrounds and in their daily life. In addition to racism, there is discrimination on the basis of language and religion from other Asian communities. Some managers prefer to appoint staff from within their own language and religious groups.

Sexism

In addition to racial discrimination, Sikh women also experience sexism. It does not necessarily manifest itself only in an anti-woman attitude. Men can also be condescending and patronising towards women, implying that a woman is not to be taken seriously as a person in her own right or her work acknowledged for its intrinsic worth. The experience of many Sikh women reveals that they are dominated at home by the male head of the family and seem not to have the same rights as men. At work they face similar problems to those of their white female colleagues as well as additional problems as Asians. One woman manager said that she supervised four Asian men and it was very difficult, as they found it hard to accept her authority. Another respondent said that Asian men held the most senior positions and still prac-tised the managerial style that they would have used in India and Pakistan.

Sikh women are increasingly seeking to choose the person they want to be, rather than following the pattern of what they are expected to be. In their domestic role, they are expected to be cooks, cleaners, child bearers and carers, looking after all the needs of the family. Their traditional role has remained the same even though they have become wage earners. The male members of the family make the decisions and females are expected to carry them out without questioning.

At work, it is hard for any women to get promotion, but it is doubly hard for Asian women. One Sikh woman said, 'It is a hard fact that you retire on the same scale you are appointed on.' Another woman commented, 'The qualifications, experience and ability of black women are not counted, they prefer to appoint men to senior positions from within Asian communities'. A workshop conducted by Sikh women on career prospects sug-gested that until recently most strategic posts in the local authorities were given to Asian men.

Men often undermine women. One woman working with young Asians told me her story. Unemployment was high in the inner city area where she worked and young Asian people had nothing to do, so a working group was set up to plan activities for young Asian girls. She was not allowed to participate, while her white boss, who knew nothing about the problem, went along and sug-gested solutions which were contrary to Asian culture. A social worker recalled a discussion on the low take-up of home care by Asian women, in which her colleagues told her she was not like 'those' Asian women, but like 'themselves', a remark which she found very patronising.

One sixty-year-old said, 'It is hard for Asian women to succeed. They not only have to face racism from the white people but also prejudice from within their own communities on the basis of religion, caste, region, class and sex.' Another woman said, 'In my experience Asian men are more sexist. They will play any tactic to undermine a woman. If nothing else, they will blame her character, which is humiliating for any Asian woman, however strong she is.'

Isolation

Isolation is a problem for many Sikh women in this country. It is caused by many things: being confined to the home, language and cultural barriers, the absence of extended families, a generation gap and, for some women, the tension of living with their sons and daughters-in-law. In traditional life a Sikh woman lived in an open house with plenty of people around her and with family and relatives to support her. One woman told me that she was desperately sad when she first arrived in England. She used to cry because she knew no one with whom she could talk. Many of the others shared her feelings of isolation and emptiness. Some women took up paid work in order to overcome their isolation. A fifty-eight-year-old said that it was not only the language barrier which made one isolated, but also the cultural barrier. She was pregnant when she came here and although she could speak English she knew nobody. It was her first pregnancy. She said, 'My parents would have looked after me in the last three months of my pregnancy if I had been in India. They would have cared for me'. Here, there was no one she could go to in times of need and distress, and she became depressed.

Isolation is one of the main reasons for depression amongst Sikh women. They miss the love and support of parental and extended family and are forced into total emotional dependence on their husbands. Isolation was less of a problem for the East Africans as they came in family units, which provided them with support and company. They also organised caste-based groups and associations in order to socialise.

Most Sikh women work today and working women have less free time to spend with their neighbours and relations. Women whose circumstances do not allow them to work feel extremely isolated, being confined to their homes. Almost all elderly Sikh women suffer from language and cultural barriers which impede their joining in with the host community. Their poor English does not allow them to socialise with their neighbours. Sikh women who come from India for matrimonial purposes often have no family or friends here and have no one to go to when they need support.

One thirty-two-year-old told me that she came here after her marriage but this did not work and she was divorced. In the absence of her family she approached *gurdwaras* for support and she was disappointed. She felt so lonely that she went back to her parents in India for a while. The growing generation gap between Sikh parents and children is also causing difficulties. Sikh women do not talk about their problems to anyone because of family *izzat* and they bear their burdens in isolation. They often complain that they do everything for their in-laws' families but in return they get only criticism. Almost all early migrant women told me that they had done everything for their in-laws' families, both in terms of moral and financial support, but when they were in need themselves, no one came forward to help.

There are a number of venues where elderly Sikh women can meet. The Social Services department runs day centres for the elderly and provides transport. Day facilities are also provided by some *gurdwaras,* where women can socialise and have tea and lunch for a nominal price if this is subsidised by the council or charity. Almost all *gurdwaras* hold '*istri satsang*' (hymn singing by women) where women socialise and eat together after *kirtan.* This helps some women to cope with their isolation.

These centres may be suitable for elderly women but do not seem to cater for the needs of younger, active women who have been made redundant or retired early. Many Sikh women made the point that there should be a drop-in venue for Indian women, that offered learning and creative facilities such as computing, dancing, singing and keep fit.

Single women
The number of single women is increasing in the Sikh community, as a result of bereavement, divorce, separation or an unwillingness to marry. A widow is supposed to live with her sons, if she has any, and is completely reliant on them and the way they treat her. It is possible that her sons may not live locally, or that

she has no sons or relations to look after her. Living on her own, she can feel extremely sad and helpless on occasion. There is no one to turn to. One widowed informant told me that life in this country was very lonely. Living alone within four walls was unbearable after she had been used to living surrounded by other people. Community closeness is also weakening. Some young wives do not want their in-laws to stay with them and seldom visit them because of their work commitments or differences of opinion.

Separation and divorce have become common among Sikhs in England. Separated and divorced women are not given the respect and sympathy they deserve. It is also difficult for them to find a suitable partner because of the stigma of having been divorced and going out to socialise with men is frowned upon.

A growing number of single women are unwilling to marry unless they find a compatible companion. They have been brought up in a family environment and although they do not wish to lose contact with the Sikh community the constant bickering of women with traditional views often forces them to cut off relations. These women have become assertive and independent, after a British education that emphasises individualism. They told me that they were not willing to compromise and indicated that they would prefer to stay single unless they found a suitable partner. As the Sikh community generally does not respect these women, especially if they live on their own and adopt western ways of life, other women prefer not to socialise with them. As a result, they face problems of isolation, loneliness and disassociation from the community.

Intoxicating drinks, smoking and drugs

Intoxicants and drinking are strictly forbidden in the Sikh religion though, according to this survey, drinking has become common amongst university-educated and young women unless they are initiated Sikhs or from strict religious families. Many informants told me that they drink wine at parties. It has been observed at parties that some Sikh women also drink spirits. One young Sikh informant, talking about her university life, said, 'We enjoy our life to the full without thinking about what is right and wrong. This is the only freedom we will have in our lifetime. Drinking is common, smoking may be a trial or a one-off'. Drink may be a part of their social life, but it is not condoned or approved of. Older Sikh women generally do not drink. Smoking and drug-taking is not common. Two young women in my survey admitted to smoking, one to taking drugs and some teenagers admitted to trying drugs but not to continuing to use them.

Conclusion

Sikhs are an established community in England now and the myth of returning home has withered away. The allegiance towards families back in the Punjab has become a low priority. England is their country of origin for the younger Sikhs, and they consider it a waste of resources to send money back to the Punjab when they have no desire to return and settle there. Sikh women have worked hard to make their life cosy and comfortable. In the beginning they did menial jobs but this has changed. Those who came from India as children and had their schooling in England did not want to work with their mothers in factories, so they took on clerical and administrative jobs. In the last decade Sikh women have increasingly entered higher education and have professional jobs as doctors, opticians, chemists, solicitors, teachers, and in the private sector, such as marketing, information technology and so on.

Increasingly, women have become financially independent. Their earnings have made their lifestyle comfortable, enhanced their social life and allowed them to spend lavishly on their life cycle rites, festivals and social activities. Dowries have escalated with the increased earning power of Sikh women and marriage ceremonies have become elaborate and lavish. Festivals such as *Vaisakhi* and *Diwali* are celebrated in hired halls with live entertainment and food. Women can afford rich food and variety in cooking. They can afford to buy quality clothes from boutiques, ready-made Punjabi suits and can also afford quality fabric for *sarees* and suits. This has enhanced their lifestyle as compared with that of the early migrants.

Early migrants who have retired or been made redundant meet in centres especially set up for this purpose. They also attend ladies' *satsangs* (weekly *kirtan* sessions). Their attitudes are becoming less traditional and more accommodating – their willingness to accept changes and compromise with their children reflects this flexibility. They have also come to terms with the fact that they cannot impose their will on British-born Sikh women. They can only guide them but cannot make decisions for them. Families who are able to hold on to their Indian values and traditions are happy, whereas those whose children have moved away from traditional values seem to be less content.

Sikh parents try to be flexible in order to accommodate the needs of their British-born children, who exhibit a growing inclination towards independence. However, some women expressed their disquiet at parents who seemed to care more about the community and the community's opinions than about their children. The concept of family solidarity is changing. British-born children do not seem to respect the traditional bonds of extended families as their parents did. They prefer only the ties of close family. Young Sikh women are no longer shy and retiring. They expect the same respect from the elderly as the elderly expect from them. Similarly, they expect to be equal partners with their husbands within their marriage and in family life.

Younger Sikh women do not have the same language and cultural barriers, or an accent problem. They have been educated in a western environment and are fully acquainted with the host culture. Those who have been to school in Britain have acquired not only the local pronunciation but also the distinctive structure and vocabulary of the local dialect with appropriate intonation and gestures. With their language and cultural behaviour, they are better equipped to fit into society than most of their parents were. Young Sikh women tend to integrate more easily with the indigenous community and have consequently been influenced by British culture. This is expressed in shorter haircuts, wearing western clothes, drinking and going out socially. Financial independence and western education are making them more individualistic.

Further Reading

Bakshi, H. S. 'An approach to support services for the elderly'. In Sharma, M. L. and Dak, T. M (eds.). *Ageing in India: Challenge for the Society*. Delhi: Ajanta Publications, n.d.

Desai, R. *Indian Immigrants in Britain*. London: Oxford University Press, 1963.

Helweg, A. W. *Sikhs in England: The Development of a Migrant Community*. Delhi: Oxford University Press, 1979.

Ikram, A. *Pakistan and the Indian Heritage*. Lahore: Sang-e-meel, 1983.

Juergensmeyer, M and Barrier, N. G. (eds.) *Sikh Studies: Comparative Perspectives on a Changing Tradition*. Working papers from the Berkeley Conference on Sikh studies. Berkeley Religious Studies Series. Berkeley: Graduate Theological Union, 1979.

Sharma, S. *Lok Gitan Vich Samajik Jiwan.* Amritsar: Ravi Sahit Prakashan, 1988.

Singh, R. *The Sikh Community in Bradford.* Bradford: Bradford College, 1978.

Singh, T. *A Short History of the Sikhs.* Vol. 1 (1469-1765). Patiala: Publication Bureau, 1969.

Singh, W. *Sikhism and Punjab's Heritage.* Patiala: Punjabi University,1990.

Tatla, D. S. *The Sikh Diaspora.* London: UCL Press, 1999.

Thomas, T. *The Way of the Guru.* Milton Keynes: Open University, 1978.

Wilson, A. *Finding a Voice: Asian Women in Britain.* London: Virago Press, 1978.

5

Cultural values

Culture covers many aspects of life. It encompasses customs, traditions and beliefs produced or shared by a particular society. This chapter concentrates on the attitudes to marriage, dowry, the joint or extended family system, and folk traditions which form the bedrock of Sikh culture, as practised by Sikhs in this country today, and how they were practised in the Punjab. It is common in the Punjab for Sikhs to share Punjabi cultural traditions and beliefs in local deities and shrines, irrespective of their religions. It is not possible to describe here all the elements that make up these beliefs but those most popular with the Sikh community are discussed, for example the worship of saints, gods and goddesses, village sacred sites, faith in miracles, magical healing, superstitions, evil spirits and village rites.

Marriage

Marriage is a socially sanctioned relationship between a man and woman. Sikhs follow the Indian cultural tradition of arranged marriages, that is, marriages arranged by parents or elders in the family. The British media often confuse arranged marriages with forced marriages but this is wrong. Forced marriages are imposed on women against their will, whereas in arranged marriages, parents take into consideration the choice and views of their children in order to secure a suitable and acceptable spouse. The system of arranged marriages is considered to be good in principle and well suited to Sikh families, as the family is an integral part of their lives. Parents not only choose a partner for their children, but also take into account the suitability of the family. When looking for a husband, parents feel it important to see whether their daughter can adjust to his family, as she will be going to live in that family. The system is not static but flexible, to accommodate the changing demands of time.

Originally, women in the Punjab were married at an early age. Girls were not educated because education had no bearing on the domestic role which they would take on after marriage. It was the parents' responsibility to oversee the welfare of their daughters. They chose a family with the best interest of their daughters in mind. In traditional marriage practices, marriage was considered not only a union between two members of the opposite sex, but also a bond between two families and their communities. Beryl Dhanjal rightly pointed out that marriage in the Punjab was less of a relationship between a particular man and woman and more of an alliance between two families (1976: 112).

The other important factors associated with arranged marriages are caste and regional endogamy, *gotra* and village exogamy. It is normal practice to find a partner from a family of similar standing and status. In Britain, education and earning capacity are added to this list. Historically, in the Punjab, one was strictly obliged to marry within one's own caste. *Jat* married *Jat*; *Ramgarhia* married *Ramgarhia*; *Khatri* married *Khatri* and *Ravidasi* married *Ravidasi* (the only exceptions to this rule were *Aroras* belonging to the *Khatri* caste who married within the *gotra* and also married relations such as cousins. These are called hypogamous marriages). The idea behind these traditions was to make any adjustment easier for daughters because of similar customs and traditions, and this extension to the kinship group increased the *robh* (prestige and power) of the family.

Sikhs traditionally applied the '*gotra*' rule when arranging marriages. This rule forbids a man to marry within the four *gotras* of his family, that is to say, the *gotras* of the mother, father, grandmother and maternal grandmother. This has now changed to forbidding marriage within two *gotras*, that of the father and mother. The rule is maintained because it is believed that people are likely to be related to each other if they belong to the same *gotra* and marriage between cousins, for instance, which may have implications for passing on genetic diseases, are to be avoided.

Sikhs also maintain that marriage should not take place with someone from the same village, as relationships within the village are viewed as being those of brother and sister. Nor do Sikhs look for a husband for their daughters from the same village or family where they have married their sons. They consider this as an unacceptable exchange (*vata satha*). However, Sikhs do tend to marry within the same geographical region in India. It is convenient for parents to travel locally to see their daughters and also easy for them to hear news. And families from the same area share similar traditions, making it easier for them to get on together. Early migrants to Britain still preferred to marry their daughters within families from the same region.

Sikhs have their own biases and stereotypes about these regions. The Punjab has three regions, *Doaba*, *Majha* and *Malwa*. The *Doabians* are considered to be affectionate and traditionalists, *Malwai* Sikhs quarrelsome and less sophisticated, whereas *Majha* Sikhs are considered to be educated and have a sense of superiority, although they are thought of as rude and less hospitable. It is difficult to verify these differences, but older Sikh women often mention them.

Another important factor when arranging a marriage is family attributes, including the standing and status of the family (*khandan*). Sikhs are particular about family background when considering marriage relationships. The status of the family is based on traditional criteria, such as caste, position, region and 'got' (*gotra*), whereas 'standing' refers to the position achieved by an individual through his personal efforts and the past history of the family. Families are assessed by family prestige, wealth, education and nobleness (*sarafat*). Achievement, either of education or wealth, is highly respected and valued by the Sikh community. In England, the traditional concept of family status has also changed. Families who have become successful have taken over high standing from established families in the Punjab or East Africa. The status and standing of a family are key factors in marriage arrangements and this remains the case for families who have been able to keep the system of arranged marriages intact.

It becomes difficult to find a suitable husband or arrange a marriage if a girl's reputation is tainted. Sikh women are expected to maintain a pure personal standard, but this does not necessarily apply to Sikh men. Another important criterion in determining the status of the bride is her appearance, which ranks above her knowledge of household skills, temperament and education. Looks are important, especially to young men who now meet their brides before getting engaged. A pretty woman with a mediocre education often does better than a less attractive, highly educated and accomplished woman.

Early Sikh migrants brought the system of arranged marriages to England from the Punjab. Marriages were arranged maintaining the same traditions and values. However, there were few Sikh families in the different cities of England and it was difficult to find suitable matches from within that small community. Parents sponsored suitable matches from the Punjab for marriage alliances. This not only gave parents a wider choice but also helped them to keep the tradition intact. The practice of sponsoring matches from the Punjab continued even after Sikhs from East Africa came to the UK, though African Sikhs preferred to marry into families from East Africa. Young women were still married at the relatively early age of sixteen to eighteen. As schooling is compulsory in Britain, girls had to attend school until they turned sixteen. After that, they either worked with their mothers or with their relations in factories. Parents exerted strict control over them and they were not allowed to go out, so had little or no interaction with the wider community. Sikh women were also very conscious of their social image, as information would circulate quickly within the close-knit community. All this contributed to the continuation of well-established marriage traditions in the early period of Sikh settlement in Britain.

Sikhs in Britain were able to keep the rules of caste, *gotra* and village for many years. It was natural for Sikhs from India to maintain this tradition, but East African Sikhs, who adhered strictly to these values in Africa, also continued them in England. This strengthened the caste bonds and perpetuated the traditional values. Bhachu points out that traditionally-arranged endogamous marriages helped group formation and the development of the community along caste lines, and also led to the perpetuation of the traditional values with which they had migrated (1985:7).

Many Sikh women favour this arrangement. The reasons given are that it is prestigious for them and their parents, making them able to keep family support and cultural affinity. A twenty-three-year-old graduate said, 'I will marry in my own caste and religion. It makes life easy and I know what is expected of me'. One twenty-year-old young woman said, 'Choosing your own partner outside your caste and religion would make you a black sheep in the community, which is far worse than pursuing your own happiness'. One sixty-eight-year-old told me that because her two daughters had married outside the Sikh religion she could hardly face the community and whenever she went out she was mocked and subjected to sarcastic and hurtful remarks which made her ill and depressed. Another woman said that the Sikh community 'makes you feel stupid and isolated' if your children marry outside your religion and culture. One woman said that mothers would not let their children talk to her, saying that she would spoil them since her daughter had married a *gora* (white man). A nineteen-year-old university student told me, 'It is not worth taking the risk of making your own choice for marriage and losing family support. In case of any problem where would I go?' Sikh women are family-oriented and it is hard for them to consider losing this support.

At the same time, one twenty-two-year-old university student suggested that arranged marriages were a gamble but that it was worth taking the risk in order to have the full backing of the family. A twenty-seven-year-old woman working away from home said she would like to have an arranged marriage as her other brothers and sisters had done so and they were happy. She added that some of her white friends were always grumbling and moaning and did not seem to be happy, despite having made their own choices. One graduate of twenty-two said, 'I want to marry in my own religion and caste. There is lot of difference between Eastern and Western culture. Also, our community disapproves of mixed marriages and you lose respect with your extended family and community thus making you isolated. I do not want to end up in this situation.'

Despite this general approval of arranged marriages, the lifestyle of Sikh families in the last forty years has changed tremendously and this has affected the attitudes and thinking of Sikh children and parents. Sikh children born, brought up and educated in England are influenced by British education and culture, values and norms, which differ from those of Eastern culture. Sikh women are now better educated and are often in employment, which entails interacting with the wider community. The Western media also exert an influence on their lives.

Life has also changed in the Punjab. Women are no longer married at such an early age and they are educated, with many going into higher education. With all these influences, it is natural for change to take place. Sikhs are adaptable and flexible when it comes to family life. In order to strengthen family relations, they make compromises even when these affect their traditional values. Parents have now begun to consult their daughters over matrimonial alliances, and decisions are made jointly. Some Sikh women have even chosen their own partners. The importance of caste, region, *gotra* and village in arranged marriages has also been affected.

Caste has traditionally been a major factor in marriage arrangements in England. However, there is a steady but growing trend for British-born Sikhs to marry across the castes. There were women in this survey whose daughters, following the teaching that there is no caste system within Sikhism, have made inter-caste marriages. One informant told me that her parents' only stipulation was that she should go out only with Sikh boys. At college she met a Sikh boy and fell in love. She did not think that there would be a problem marrying him, as he was a Sikh. When her parents found out that he belonged to the 'water-carrier' (*jhir*) caste they told her not to see him any more. She told me she has been disgusted by her parents' comments and their claim that they belonged to the *Jat* caste (an agricultural grouping and supposedly superior to other Sikhs). She told me that she had had a civil marriage in spite of parental opposition and that both families and the Sikh community had consequently rejected her. In the end, she had had no choice but to leave home as communication broke down completely with her parents and even now there is no chance of reconciliation. She said she felt frustrated at the duality of Sikh behaviour where one thing is said and another done. 'How can they expect respect from the younger generation if they themselves do not practice the very basic principles of Sikhism?' This incident took place some ten years ago and is not an isolated case.

Until recently, marriages outside one's caste but within the Sikh religion were rarely accepted and blessed by parents. Now there is a growing trend towards inter-caste marriages and Sikh parents have reluctantly begun to accept them. Marriages have taken place even between the highest and lowest castes. This may have little to do with Sikhism but more with a general weakening of the caste system and its relevance in western and urbanised environments, where it has little or no significance beyond marriage. On observation, it seems likely that, for Sikhs in the future, caste will become much less important, thus paving the way for genuine Sikh tenets to be followed.

Inter-*gotra* marriages on the other hand are still considered socially unacceptable and are talked about frequently. Sikhs are hesitant about marrying within their own *gotra* and there are few exceptions to this rule. I once witnessed an inter-*gotra* love marriage that was condemned by relatives and friends throughout the ceremony because they were offended by the closeness of the relationship. People said, 'Is she wedding a brother or a cousin?'

The traditional requirement to marry within the region from which one's ancestors came in the Punjab has no significance for younger generation Sikhs in Britain and this practice has died out. Nor do British-born Sikhs, educated here, give the same importance to the traditional concept of family status. There is a growing emphasis on the standing, rather than the status, of the family. Young people are keen to have a compatible partner, rather than a partner of high family status who may be incompatible. These days, personal achievements and good conduct receive preference over family attributes. A young woman with qualifications and good conduct is preferred to one with family status only. Much more importance is given to attributes such as earning potential, education and social manners. All these far outweigh the family's ancestry and present position. In many cases, choices centre on the individual rather than the family, especially as better-educated young women emerge through the university and higher education system in England.

Educated women are also keen to have compatibility with their husbands, which they consider essential for a successful personal and professional life. They wish to have much more say in the selection of their marriage partners. In the past, many women suffered in silence because of incompatible marriage partners. One informant with a postgraduate degree spoke about her arranged marriage with a man who had not even studied to matriculation level. She openly admitted that every minute of the day was a disaster because she had nothing in common with her husband. She had never felt that she was his wife or partner, merely his cook and cleaner. Her nights were empty and she could never be emotionally involved with him. This may be an exceptional case but there are many instances of incompatible couples in this survey.

One fifty-nine-year-old told me that she was better educated than her husband but he always tried to make her look small in front of other women and would call her stupid. A forty-seven-year-old obsewrved that she had worked very hard, gained further qualifications and secured a prestigious job, whereas her husband was still doing the same job. She said she had nothing in common with him. She could not discuss anything with him, as he did not understand her problems. There were other young Sikh women in the survey who had no hesitation in revealing their inner feelings. One twenty-nine-year-old woman said, 'I wanted to run away rather than enter an arranged marriage without knowing my life partner'. A twenty-four-year-old woman said, 'Arranged marriages are like a cattle market, fixing a match without knowing each other'.

A twenty-six-year-old woman said, 'I do not totally approve of arranged marriages. This is a gamble. You start a life with a total stranger. It is like legalised prostitution, you live with a person without knowing him and sleep with a man without emotional involvement'. Another woman told me that she did not believe in arranged marriages. Her husband was impotent and she felt that she had been deceived and her life was ruined. One twenty-two-year-old said that she came from India to marry, but had been married to a man who was already living with a *gori*. He had never cared for her and spent most of his time with the other woman. His family treated her like a servant and also made her give her wages to her mother-in-law. She stayed with the family for two years and then left.

Although most marriages are between two Sikhs, love marriages with non-Sikhs are not uncommon and these are termed mixed marriages. Contributory factors are the changing lifestyle of the younger generation and their growing interaction with the wider community. Their common identity of being British, their under-standing of British traditions and values, the irrelevance of some of their own traditions and values within a new geographical environment and the reluctance on the part of the Sikh com-munity to adapt to new ways, all lead to unions with non-Sikhs.

Mixed marriages should be defined within this context. Inter-religious and interracial marriages are considered to be mixed marriages and these are frowned on by the Sikh community. They are not easily condoned by even educated and professional Sikhs, although marriages with Hindus are reluctantly accepted.

Some *gurdwaras* do not perform such wedding ceremonies, believing that to do so would encourage other young Sikhs. Mixed marriages are believed to be against Sikh religious tenets as stated in the *Sikh Rahit Maryada*, though the Sikh religion makes no discrimination on the basis of caste, creed and colour, and such marriages take place without parental blessing. Parents do not support the majority of these marriages and there is often no representation from the bride's side at the wedding, though some parents do reluctantly join in.

There was a time when children who went down this path were completely ostracised. Their parents totally rejected them and they became the forgotten children. These marriages were kept secret and parents avoided disclosing them to the community. The situation of most women in mixed marriages has changed in recent years, however, and now they should be able to maintain some kind of relationship with their parents, perhaps not immediately, but at least after a year or two, although the Sikh community gives them no respect and their presence at functions is resented. Extended families seldom invite them to functions, in the belief that the other children will be influenced.

One fifty-eight-year-old woman told me that her husband had stopped her daughter coming home because she was living with a *gora*. The mother was trying to maintain communication with her daughter in the hope that she would bring her round to the Sikh culture. One sixty-five-year-old told me that her daughter married a Gujarati and her husband stopped her coming home. Her husband is now dead but she still wants to honour his wishes. So, on the occasion of her son's marriage, she told him that she would not be responsible for inviting his sister to his wedding, but that he could invite her if he wanted to. There are some instances in the survey where parents who once had no connection with their daughters are now being reconciled with them. One mother told me that her daughter went astray, lost the support of her family and went through a difficult period, but that once she was reconciled with her family, she settled down again. The mother added that the family had had to pay the price of their conservative thinking, having placed too much importance on family *izzat* and image in the community.

Some young women have reluctantly had to end love affairs because of pressure from their parents. One informant said that Sikhs gave preference to the community rather than to their own families. A twenty-six-year-old woman commented that Sikh children born and brought up here live in a culture weakened by contact with British values but that they could conveniently cope with either culture. She believed that the important element in the marriage arrangements should be suitability and compatibility rather than caste and religion. She asked me, 'How many girls are Sikhs by conviction? They are Sikhs only by birth'. This is supported by the survey conducted in Leeds, which suggests that few families truly practice Sikhism and that there are few Sikh women who have a thorough understanding of Sikh religious tenets. However, a university graduate who does pointed out a possible discrepancy in the prescription of the *Sikh Rahit Maryada* that a Sikh woman should necessarily marry a Sikh man. She said that it is stated in the *Guru Granth Sahib* that a man should be known by his deeds, not by his caste or religion. This disturbed her, because she had studied Sikhism closely and would prefer to lead her life according to her understanding of the religion.

The Sikh community exerts pressure in its own way to put a stop to mixed marriages. Women who have had mixed marriages are unwelcome in the community. A twenty-nine-year-old woman who had married a *gora* told me that she took her newborn daughter to the *gurdwara* to have a naming ceremony, but was horrified at the comments other women made about her husband. Her husband liked going to the *gurdwara* as he enjoyed *kirtan* (hymn singing). A thirty-five-year-old woman who married a *gora* told me that she knew that she was not welcome in the *gurdwara*, but also knew that no one could stop her going there. As anyone can go to the *gurdwara* irrespective of their religion and colour, she goes there regularly with her three children.

Women in this survey who had opted for a mixed marriage were found to be happy with their lives. Their only regret was losing the support of their family and being isolated from the Sikh community. A thirty-eight-year-old said that she had two sisters-in-law, one married to a Sikh and the other to a *gora*. The one who married a Sikh was always grumbling when she came to visit her and the one who married a *gora* was always laughing and bubbly. This woman was afraid that the obvious difference between these two marriages would give her young children the impression that marriage with a Sikh is unlikely to be happy. One woman who had a mixed marriage was asked, 'Do you think it is worth it, when you are losing something so dear (her family) to you?' Her reply was, 'Love is not intentional, it just happens. Sikhs call it *sanyog* (destiny). If it was not destined why did we come here?' Another said that she was extremely happy and led a full life. Her husband and his family were caring, and this enabled her to make a success of her career too. One newly-married twenty-five-year-old woman said that people should learn to accept individuals on their merits and not for their caste, colour or religion.

Mixed marriages are a product of the interaction of different cultures and of men and women having a wider choice. The increase in such marriages is slow but steady and indicates a future trend towards self-choice. These marriages usually happen among women keen to make their own decisions in a search for compatibility and suitability, or women frustrated by the system. One young woman made a mixed marriage simply because her maternal uncle wanted her to marry a man from India whom she disliked. She tried to talk to her mother, but to no avail, so she ran away. As the Sikh community does not accept 'runaway' women, she ended up marrying a white man. A professional woman told me that many Sikh families have no concept of the demands their work imposes on professional women. There are also few middle class educated families, which makes it difficult to find a suitable match from within that narrow choice. One woman related her experience of finding a suitable match for her professional daughter, saying that there were few families with moderate views – most were either fanatic and orthodox or very westernised.

Divorce and separation

Whereas arranged marriages lasted well in the past, they do not seem to work so successfully now. Divorce and separation are increasing. The British media have blamed the system of arranged marriages, but it is not that simple. Sikh marriages survived before for many reasons, such as strong information networks, early marriage, the role of women as housewives, the lack of education for women, the concept of *izzat*, financial dependency on men and women's acceptance of the *status quo*. Information about prospective partners passed from family to family was also significant in making marriages work. Originally, arranged marriages took place within families already known to one another. Women would arrange marriages by bringing their own sisters, nieces and other relations to the families into which they themselves had married. Parents normally knew the family personally or through their relations. They could find out much information about the man and his family through networking. When Sikhs started migrating or moving away from their villages and areas because of industrialisation and urbanisation, this weakened the information-finding network they had had in the Punjab. It became difficult to find the information they needed to make an appropriate and informed decision.

Sikh women are becoming educated, financially independent and more confident about making decisions for themselves. Financial independence and education have made them unwilling to make unnecessary compromises or accept unreasonable pressure or behaviour from their husband or in-laws. Western education encourages people to question. All this has contributed to an enormous change from the traditional behaviour of Sikh women. Furthermore, they are no longer willing to be submissive and tolerant for the sake of family *izzat*. One forty-three-year-old told me that her husband was an alcoholic and a gambler. This had been going on for twenty-five years and his family had kept her busy, allowing her little time to find out about his activities. Now that she had discovered the truth and wanted to be separated from her husband, her mother had begged her to save family *izzat* and had asked her to stay with him, as she had already been married for so long, but she had decided to leave him. Another woman told me that her husband was aggressive and violent and used to beat her. Finally, she could not take any more and left him. A twenty-six-year-old professional woman said, 'I divorced my husband because he was violent and had had an extra-marital affair'. Other women, however, continue to suffer in silence. One thirty-eight-year-old said that she knew about her husband's extra-marital affair, but she would not separate from him because of her children.

The changing role of women, combining work and domestic life, is also a contributory factor to dissatisfaction. The demands on women's time are different from what they used to be. They need support from their husbands in running the home and looking after children and want to be treated as equal partners. In traditional families, the changing role of women as wage earners is not fully appreciated. Working women often need to meet people in their professional capacity and to attend meetings at unsociable hours. Conservative husbands and families put undue pressure on women and, in certain cases, accuse them of having loose characters. Under such circumstances, marriages often break down. One thirty-three-year-old told me that her father-in-law called her a whore, simply because he could not understand her attendance at meetings held in the evening.

Mismatch within arranged marriages also causes failure of Sikh marriages. When a woman cannot find a suitable match in England, her parents look to India or Africa, and men do the same. Parents often prefer to send their children abroad where they can find better-educated partners from good families. The resultant lack of parental support, possible incompatibility and adjustment to a new cultural environment can place pressure on such marriages and lead to separation or divorce.

Divorced women do not seem to have the same lowly position in society as they had before, because of their financial independence, but the structure of Sikh society has not allowed them much freedom of movement. One divorced woman in her thirties told me that her Sikh neighbours frowned upon her if she went out for meals or to see a film with friends.

Despite these difficulties, most young women in this survey are in favour of arranged marriages so as to retain the support of their families, which is not only a source of strength but also gives them security in times of distress. However, many suggested that they would like to see far more flexibility and choice within the system. It is important that they should also have the choice to date and reject potential partners. The number of educated women is growing and, with that growth, the question of compatibility is becoming increasingly important. Parents are happy to accept their children's choice when it conforms to caste and *gotra* rules, and have also began to accept, albeit reluctantly, inter-caste marriages, as long as these are within their own religion.

Thus, it is likely that arranged marriages that allow self-choice from within the Sikh community will be the future norm of Sikh marriages. Some marriages with non-Sikhs will always take place in spite of parental and community disapproval. It is impossible to put a stop to mixed marriages as Sikh women enter into demanding careers and meet compatible men from religions and cultures other than their own. Sikh parents will have to become more flexible in order to sustain the tradition of arranged marriages.

Dowry

Daaj (dowry) as applied to the Sikh community in the Punjab, is the tradition of giving gifts or presents to the daughter at the time of her leaving the parental home at marriage. These gifts usually conform to the social norms of the time. The giving of a dowry is a sign of the affection shown by the parental family, but it can become a burden if parents do not have enough money to fulfil the dowry requirements expected of them. This practice is common in the Punjab and it forms a part of the Indian culture, although different religions and regions have interpreted it in their own ways. In some regions of North India, an amount of money is fixed before the engagement and the marriage ceremony will not take place unless that fixed amount is paid. Although the Punjab is a part of North India, the concept of dowry there is different. No money is asked for in the dowry and generally no dowry is fixed in marriage transactions. Sikhs follow social norms about dowry that are normally taken as a guide to what to give to their daughters in marriage. The dowry is given by the 'bride givers' without expecting a return, and it is the right of the 'bride takers' to be the recipients.

The dowry is given to Sikh girls according to social convention and family wealth makes it a matter of prestige that rich parents always give much more than social norms dictate. It is believed within the Sikh community that the *daaj* is important for a girl in order to have the respect of her in-laws' family, though Sikh religious dictates suggest that neither a woman nor a man should be married for money. The tradition in earlier days was that girls were married as adolescents and whatsoever was given in marriage then belonged to the in-laws. Whatever was given at the time of *muklava* (the sending of a married woman to her in-laws' home when she became an adult) belonged to the woman. When the pattern of age changed and women began to get married later, the period spent with their parents between marriage and *muklava* became unnecessary. Nowadays, the *daaj* given to daughters at the time of their marriage belongs to them and has four main components. The first three are exclusively for the bride and the fourth is for the groom, his family and relations.

The first component consists of items of clothing for the bride – suits of good quality material and *sarees*. In the 1960s it was five suits and later on this became seven, nine and then eleven. At present, the norm is twenty-one or even more suits and *sarees*. Normally, the clothes given to the bride are silk suits with heavy embroidery, designer suits and new fashions like *lehgha choli*, which are much more expensive than ordinary suits.

The second component of *daaj* is gold, which the bride receives from her family. It used to be earrings and a ring for the bride in the 1950s. In the 1960s, it became usual to give a set – earrings, a necklace and a ring. Rich parents occasionally added a pair of bangles or *gajre*. The maternal uncle gave *natth* (nose jewellery). It is normal these days to give on average 20-35 *tolas* (approximately 8-14 ounces) of gold. Some wealthy parents give diamonds, pearls and other expensive stones set in gold.

The third part of the dowry consists of household goods, including utensils, crockery, kitchen gadgets, linen, quilts, furniture and items such as sewing machines, washing machines, dishwashers and stereos. In the 1960s it would be utensils, crockery, kitchen gadgets, linen, quilts and a sewing machine along with small household presents. Sewing machines have become less popular and are optional now but there is an increase in goods such as irons, radios and food-mixers. Items such as washing machines and dishwashers are also becoming common because of the increased earning power of women.

The fourth component relates to the gifts received by the groom's family and close relations. The groom normally receives two suits, one woollen and one cotton or polyester, a gold *kara* (bangle), a ring and a watch. The suit includes a shirt, shoes and socks. Some also receive a gold chain and bracelet. The groom's mother receives two to five unsewn pieces of clothing (*salwar, kameez* and *dupatta*) or *sarees* and some gold. The present norm is five suits and earrings or a chain. Some families give one gold set to the mother-in-law. The groom's father also receives a suit, gold ring and blanket, with some money (£101 or less) on *vaidaygi*, which is when the bride leaves her parental home after the marriage ceremony.

Other relations receive presents in the form of clothes and gold jewellery, along with a nominal amount of money (£5 or £11). The groom's extended family also receives unsewn suits, men's shirts or turbans and some money (£5 or £10). Among the recipients are paternal grandparents (*dada, dadi*) and maternal grandparents (*nana, nani*), maternal uncles and aunts (*masi, masad, mami, mama*) and finally paternal uncles and aunts (*chacha, chachi, taya, tayi*, and *bhua, phuphar*). Grandparents sometimes receive preferential treatment and are given jewellery as well as suits.

These are common customs followed by the Sikh community in England. Some families are known to have given cars and cash deposits for houses to their daughters. Wealthy families do not restrict themselves to the prevailing social customs. They try to reflect their wealth in the amount of dowry they give to their daughters. Dowry is always generous, because it is a status confirmer and much talked about within the community. It is felt by some in the Sikh community that the level of dowries is getting out of control in England and some organisations such as those associated with the *Bhatras* and *Ramgarhias* have taken steps to produce guidelines to keep the amount of dowry under control.

Dowry is not demanded or asked for in the Sikh community, but it has become obligatory. I did not come across a single woman who had been married without a *daaj*. This is simply because her position would have been vulnerable in her marital home if she had arrived without one, or with one less than that dictated by social conventions. A marriage without a *daaj* would also reflect badly on family status and *izzat*.

One woman told me that her husband did not like the tradition of *daaj* and he thought it a disgrace to give or receive *daaj*. He told his in-laws that his only condition of marriage was that there should be no *daaj*. The girl's parents were educated and socially well off but did not know what to do. Eventually they decided to give clothes and gold to the daughter, her prospective husband and his family, suggesting to the bridegroom that these were the immediate necessities for the bride and it was not a *daaj*. They did not give other things like crockery, utensils, bedding or furniture. After thirty three years of marriage, this woman vividly recalls every cruel word said to her by her in-laws and how badly they had treated her, constantly saying that she came from a poor family and that her father could not afford to give her even a *kowli* (soup plate). Her sister-in-law would insult her on every possible occasion.

At the same time, families are frowned upon if they ask for *daaj*. There is general disapproval attached to any demands made by the groom's side for a sum of money or particular gifts as a price for the groom. There were two families in this survey whose daughters were asked to bring specific amounts of money to buy a car or a house after marriage. News of such demands travels fast in the community, placing the groom's family in an embarrassing situation. This may have negative consequences, as women from good families will no longer be suggested for these men. In fact, most families take pride in emphasising that they have no interest in *daaj*. Although it is shameful to ask for a dowry, it is common for women from the in-laws' family to bicker over petty matters of colour, print and quality of suits and sometimes over the quantity given.

Daaj is given and received despite the disapproval of the Sikh religion and has been on the increase since the 1960s. To me it appears that the earning power of working women has made *daaj* more elaborate. It is normal for a working woman to add her own earnings into the *daaj*, investing her money in what is eventually going to be hers. Most Sikh parents will not accept money earned by their daughters, but their daughters can spend their own money and what they take with them at the time of their marriage. The improvement in quality and increase in volume of certain components of *daaj* are undoubtedly linked to the earning power of brides themselves, family wealth and the woman's position within the family. It all helps women enormously if they want to set up their own home soon after marriage. Young women who have not gone out to work get comparatively less *daaj*, as do women coming from India who bring less *daaj* with them because of weight restrictions on the airlines.

Increased *daaj* helps a woman set up home, but it may also put undue pressure on the parents. It works for families with one or two daughters but not for those with many daughters. Nor does it suit parents who are paying to put their daughters through higher education. By the time a woman finishes her education there is little time left for earning before she is likely to be married. It then becomes a burden for parents to fulfil the social norms of the dowry. This survey revealed that some bright girls were not allowed to go into higher education simply because their parents wanted them to work for two to three years to save for their *daaj*. The opinions of young Sikh women are divided on this matter. Some said that this was their tradition and it should be continued, but one nineteen-year-old said that when two individuals were getting married what was the need for a dowry?

In general, dowries have not caused major problems within the Sikh community, except for a few exceptions where women have been pressurised to bring money or expensive items. Most families are happy if the social conventions are met.

Joint family system

Sikhs believe in a joint family system. The 'joint family' originally meant a family sharing a common residence, a common kitchen and a common purse. The head of a joint or extended family is the eldest living male. The joint family includes parents, sons and their wives, grandchildren and unmarried daughters. Sometimes there is an extension of the joint family to include some of the man's other relations. They will all live in a single household, eating together and maintaining a common pantry. Property is held jointly and resources pooled. Decisions are made communally, but final authority rests with the head of the household. Each person is expected to do his or her duty according to their age, education and position in Sikh society and children must show respect to their parents and older relations. This is the ideal, but not all families have identical systems. Joint living can take three forms: where both generations are living together, where married brothers are living in the same household, or a combination of the two.

Joint families have always been the norm in the Punjab. The head of the family would make decisions that were accepted by the rest of the family. The village economy was based on agriculture and family labour upheld the system, but pressure on land forced some family members to leave their village. New technologies impoverished the village cottage industries, forcing workers to seek new opportunities in the cities, while others ventured out for economic and political reasons. In India, mobility increased after the Second World War. Increasing numbers moved out of villages and into the cities, both in India and abroad, where they set up businesses or entered the labour market to earn wages. Industrialisation and urbanisation reduced the number of extended families, and this has given rise to drastic changes in the organisation of the joint family at domestic level.

The family pattern in the UK is mainly nuclear, but there are also some families in a variety of joint living arrangements. I found families with three generations living under one roof: elderly parents, sons and their wives, grandsons and their wives and unmarried grandsons and daughters. In other families sons and their wives live with elderly parents – a common pattern. When one son gets married he will live with the family until the next brother marries. Parents will then suggest that their elder son buys his own house. One of the reasons for asking the son to buy his house is that houses in many industrial towns are not designed to accommodate large families. If a brother does not get along well with the family, he is asked to live separately.

Another common model of joint living involves buying houses next door to each other. The sons sleep in their own houses with their families but the kitchen is shared and the joint family spend much time together. Grandparents look after young children. It is a Sikh tradition that parents live with their sons and not with their daughters. The Sikh community strictly observes this tradition. It is a son's responsibility to look after his elderly parents and this is one reason why a son is preferred to a daughter. Daughters have to leave the parental home after marriage, whereas sons have to stay with their parents. They not only look after their parents but also contribute to the marriages of their sisters. Even brothers who live separately contribute to common family expenses such as a sister's wedding. Economies of scale that are achieved by an undivided joint family have reinforced the idea of a family all living together as the ideal.

In the Punjab, a son had no effective opportunity to break away from his family, since income was pooled and derived mainly from the land. Access to land could only be achieved by in-heritance, so a son had no alternative but to live with his family. The situation in England is very different, as Sikh men and women have their own incomes. They are independent wage earners, except where there is a common family business. Business ventures are often cooperative affairs, involving family and relatives, so the joint family remains an ideal system in these cases.

Sikh women are divided on the matter of joint living. Those who favoured living in a joint family gave reasons such as shared living costs, help with child-care, general support, sharing of domestic work and company for shopping and outings. In this survey, many young married women said that it was beneficial for them to stay in a joint family so that they could get to know other family members and also to understand family customs. It gave them the opportunity to study further, to take up a job without worrying about child care and also to save money to buy their own house in the future if they wished to do so.

The women who do not favour joint living say that it is an intrusion into privacy and independence. The main criticisms of joint families which emerged from the survey are resentment, fault-finding, rejection, criticism and unnecessary interference. Some women also cited bickering, restrictions, constraints and being closely watched.

There are families in the survey for whom the system has not worked very well. The women involved gave various reasons for this. Sometimes wives in joint families may not get along with each other, as they are strangers to one another, originate from different families and may have different priorities. Some families have poor communication and disagree over petty matters and some families simply fail to compromise. One thirty-one-year-old woman said that there was no appreciation for her work for the family, only criticism. A forty-eight-year-old woman said, 'You do everything for them and they exploit you. My brother-in-law took everything we had jointly in the Punjab'. Another thirty-year-old said that there was no family loyalty. 'They come to you when they need something, otherwise they do not care'.

Another factor, often expressed by younger professional women, is incompatibility. There is bound to be tension in less compatible families when, for example, a professional woman has married into a conservative and uneducated family and where the demands of her job are not recognised and met. One professional informant told me that her sister-in-law, who worked as a packer, used to say that the informant could not be tired as she sat on a chair all day. Her sister-in-law did not think that mental work and a professional job could be tiring. The woman's in-laws expected her to do everything in the house for them because her job was not physical and therefore not tiring. Women in professional jobs often need to take further qualifications or undertake courses to progress in their careers. This is difficult in incompatible families where their needs are disregarded. Lack of privacy is also seen to be a problem, especially by young women. One told me that the grandmother from her in-laws' family had cleaned her bedroom and had gone through her drawers.

Families in Britain who live jointly are not living under any compulsion, but share a house of their own free will. The joint family system works well in compatible families where the head of the family is just and fair. It also works in business families, who often live jointly because of pooled resources and demands on their time.

A joint residence may no longer be practical but this has by no means destroyed the concept of joint families. Sikh families may not live in a joint residence for many reasons such as migration, moving away, smaller houses or differences of opinion, but they do not ignore their obligations to their families. They may not share a common purse, but the obligation of a son to obey and support his father and the obligation of brothers to cooperate is often preserved. Many informants in my survey told me that they send money regularly to their husbands' families in India. Such remittances not only increase the Indian family resources but also fulfil the obligation of a son towards his family. It is common practice among Sikh families to send substantial amounts of money on occasions such as weddings in the family, renovating houses or buying new properties. Some women also told me that they had sent air tickets to bring their family members here and supported them until they got jobs and houses. Sikh families also help each other financially when buying houses, setting up businesses or with other major expenses.

The joint family is a combination of many relationships. Matrilineal relations are often considered to be generally sympathetic, loving, cooperative and caring. Patrilineal relations on the other hand are often felt to lack such attributes, particularly where relations with sisters-in-law (*nanan, bharjayi, darani, jathani*) and mothers-in-law are concerned. Women who do not have their own family close by are often undermined and abused. One fifty-eight-year-old woman told me that she came from India after her marriage and did not have any patrilineal relations in this country. She had done a great deal for her in-laws' family, such as looking after her husband's brother and bearing all the expenses of his wedding, sending air tickets for his nephews and contributing to the marriages of his sisters' and brothers' children. She wept when she said that despite this they were always critical of her and constantly undermined her.

Thus the joint family system can have both positive and negative effects. For example, a woman who has other relatives in the family she has married into will be in a stronger position than the rest of women in that family. She can dominate the family and exercise her *robh* (power) because of the support of her relations. Consultation and fairness are key elements for a joint family system but they fade in the glare of family prestige. Two informants in the survey told me that their husbands were having affairs. Their in-laws did not blame their sons, suggesting instead that the women might be lacking in some way and failing to satisfy their husbands. Both the women felt so frustrated that one finally divorced her husband and the other returned to her husband just to take revenge on his parents. One divorced woman told me that her husband was an alcoholic and went out with *goris* (white women). Her in-laws, rather than giving her support, had accused her of having a disreputable character.

In spite of such difficulties, the family takes precedence over individuals. On the whole, there is a great deal of respect for elderly parents, whether families live in a shared residence or separately. It is at critical points, particularly at births, marriages and deaths, that the unity of families can clearly be seen. All the members of the immediate family will come together to make their contributions for entertaining guests, for the dowry, or to receive the commiseration of others. Showing their unity on such occasions is important for family prestige. Young Sikhs are ingrained with such values even if they want to live independently. My survey found that even family members in dispute, and not generally on speaking terms, would join together on family occasions.

In joint families that do work well, members stress mutual respect and obligations towards one another. Although the head of the family is the final decision maker, he will consult every member of the family. The stability of the joint family is grounded as much in mutual obligation as upon the unilateral exercise of authority. This survey showed that although the elderly may not have the same authority as they do in the Punjab, they are nevertheless listened to and their advice sought. Many young Sikh women told me that they take pride in family unity and solidarity. As the family is a source of support and strength in the Sikh community, Sikhs retain their allegiance to it at almost any cost. Thus they make immense effort to choose appropriate families for marriage purposes, in order to make their joint and extended families stable and strong.

In the western and urbanised environment, there are forces in the generational, cultural and educational realm which create divisions, but these are countered by family love, loyalty and security. The family is central to Sikh women. The importance of looking after parents in their later years is instilled in sons. Leaving elderly parents in old people's homes is considered a disgrace to the family. In Britain, many young couples are used to, and value, greater independence than joint family living permits, but it is still common for some young couples to spend the first few years of their married life with the husband's parents.

Although most Sikh children believe in looking after their parents, some elderly Punjabis felt that the attitudes of their sons and daughters-in-law were changing. One elderly woman told me that her young daughter-in-law did not care for her and was not willing to listen to her advice. However, when I interviewed her daughter-in-law, she told me, 'I go to work early in the morning and come home late. I feel exhausted, as my job is demanding. My mother in-law complains and moans when I come home.' She felt that that her mother-in-law was not only demanding but also failed to understand her situation.

Some elderly parents feel they are being used to look after the home and take care of children while their daughters-in-law are working. One seventy-two-year-old told me that she had looked after her grandchildren, and cooked and cleaned while her daughter-in-law was at work. Now that the grandchildren are grown up, she feels that her daughter-in-law does not give her the same respect and love as she did before.

The elderly who stay at home all day often feel lonely and can be isolated because of language barriers. Some women said they had lost contact with their children, because the children have become extremely westernised in their behaviour and thinking. Some of these women live alone in their own houses or in council flats. There may be no support within the joint or extended families, but in Leeds there is provision for elderly Sikhs to meet together at different venues, creating an alternative support system. They meet at religious places like *gurdwaras*, and also at day centres opened and funded by Social Services. Facilities of this kind are available in towns such as Birmingham, Coventry, Derby and many boroughs of London. These places organise programmes for them, particularly shopping, outings, keep-fit, swimming and invite guest speakers to speak on topics of interest and health issues.

A number of contributory factors give rise to feelings of isolation, such as a greater gap of understanding between the generations, the economic independence of women, little spare time because both partners are working, the influence of a woman's family living in close proximity and the concept of self-help.

Some younger Sikhs may not want to live with their parents but that does not imply that they want no contact with them. The expectations of many of the elderly were shaped in the Punjab and are difficult to meet within the new cultural environment. The effect of western values is also making young Sikhs less tolerant and accommodating, thus creating a barrier between generations.

Folk traditions and beliefs

Punjabis believe in folk traditions that have evolved over centuries. The Punjab was a gateway into India, so many people settled there, bringing their own religions, culture and traditions.

Settlers not only adopted existing traditions but also influenced them, and this gave birth to new ones. Punjabi folk traditions are thus a fusion of many cultures and traditions, not necessarily akin to Sikh traditions. Sikh women from the Punjab are more susceptible than East African or British-born Sikhs to Punjabi cultural influences and customs, and the influence of local traditions, such as worshipping at shrines and belief in deities and evil spirits, remains dominant in their way of life. Rural Sikh women practised these traditions in the Punjab and carried them abroad when they migrated, passing them on to their daughters and daughters-in-law.

Superstitions

Certain popular superstitions exist in different parts of the Punjab. These are generally passed on orally and play a significant role in women's lives. Some of the superstitions mentioned by my interviewees are listed below:

- If an owl stands on the roof of a house, it is a symbol of illness or death in that house.

- Hair and clothes should not be washed on a Tuesday or a Thursday, as this brings bad luck.

- It is important to consult Brahmans or astrologers to find an auspicious day and date for fixing marriages or other happy occasions.

- If a black cat crosses your path when you are on your way somewhere, you will not be successful in your mission.

- Meeting a Brahman or a widow is not a good omen.

- A widow should not be allowed to participate in any important ceremonies or occasions.

- One should not go into a kitchen wearing shoes. There will not be *barkat* (prosperity) in the house if one cooks food bareheaded.

- Hair should not be combed in the evening.

- The house should not be swept in the evening and one should not put out rubbish in the evening.

- One should not do any embroidery in the evening as it hurts the eyes of birds.

- Vegetables and flowers should not be gathered after sunset as the plants are believed to be resting.

- It is considered ominous to sneeze when someone is departing, or at the start of a new initiative. If this happens, the person is normally asked to wait for few minutes. If they are in a hurry, thay are given sugar to eat before leaving.

- One should not leave home at a quarter to the hour.

- One should not leave one's hair hanging over the bed while sleeping. This may not be applicable in Britain as beds have headboards, but in the Punjab *charpais* (beds made of four wooden round sticks woven with string) do not. The belief is that a snake can climb on to the hair. Similarly one should not sit on the bed with shoes on, as it tempts snakes to climb up.

- Houses which are narrow at the front and wider at the back are called cow-faced houses and are considered lucky. Houses with a wide front and narrow back are considered unlucky, as are houses overlooking a T-junction.

- One should not come in close contact with a woman who is menstruating or who has just given birth to a child (*sutak*), as they are considered to be impure.

- It is not considered auspicious for someone leaving the country or city to be faced by a woman with an empty vessel or basket.

- If a child who is breast-feeding dies, the sister-in-law (the husband's sister) will not sit among the mourners.

- If clothes are unintentionally worn the wrong way round, it suggests that someone will be released from prison.

- If a crow makes a noise on your roof, you should expect a guest. If a dog barks in front of your house, a death is expected.

- Certain numbers are considered unlucky, for example, the number 13, and a child born in *Kartik* (October-November) is not considered to be lucky for the parents.

- The colour red is believed to bring good luck. This is one reason why wedding dresses are normally red, while white is the colour of mourning.

These are some of the superstitions commonly believed by rural Sikh women. Such beliefs still influence the values of Sikhs in Britain. They believe deeply in them and pass them on to their daughters and daughters-in-law, so these superstitions have a strong hold. One woman told me that she always consulted an astrologer to fix an auspicious time for the wedding of her children. A forty-year-old woman said she would never wash her hair on Tuesdays or Thursdays. A fifty-year-old criticised another Sikh woman for having her son's birthday *path bhog* (religious reading of the holy book) during the time of *shradhs* (a time of the year when Brahmans are fed in order to respect and feed the dead ancestors), when happy occasions should not be celebrated. When I asked the reasons for their beliefs, these women could not explain them – although some stem from common sense. Wearing shoes in the kitchen, cooking bareheaded and placing shoes on the bed are discouraged simply for reasons of hygiene. Doing embroidery in the evening can ruin one's own eyesight rather than birds' eyesight and one could fall while taking out rubbish in the dark. Others may be cultural traditions evolved from the Hindu religion, such as consulting Brahmans about auspicious days and dates and the non-participation of widows (their lowly status made them unlucky) in happy occasions. Yet others may be irrational, such as washing one's hair and clothes on certain days, dislike of black cats, sneezing at certain times, or not leaving home at a quarter to the hour.

Worshipping at local shrines and deities

The teachings of the Sikh *gurus* stress the futility of worshipping at shrines but it is common for rural Sikh women to visit the shrines of Muslim *pirs* (saints), *samadhis* (tombs associated with Hindu and Sikh saints) and *jatheras* (cremation sites of village ancestors). Sikh women also practise *pitrs* or ancestor worship. Offering food to Brahmans is common in England, in order to perform *shradhs* for dead elders. This is done every year during the *shradh* period, which falls around October. The belief is that this food will reach their ancestors. Village women will also visit a shrine for *jathera*, or the common ancestor of the clan, where offerings of purified butter and flour are made on auspicious occasions in the family. These visits are also made to heal ailments and psycho-social problems, procure the birth of a son, cure cattle of diseases, resolve inter-personal conflicts and respect village rites. Women also worship *marhi massan* (graves and graveyards), the sites of cremation. After a body is burnt, the ashes are collected and a small heap or mound is made, which is plastered over with mud. Villagers mutually share these village sites for worship, particularly if they are known for granting wishes.

Many Sikh women believe in saints and undertake regular pilgrimages to the Punjab. One seventy-two-year-old told me that she went to India every year to perform *Akhand path* (the continuous reading of the *Granth*) at the place of a local saint she believed in. Many other Sikh women go there to pay a visit and donate money to saints they worship. A fifty-eight-year-old woman told me that her mother-in-law took her to every local place of worship after her marriage. She said that as a Sikh she did not believe in the value of this, but did not want to hurt her mother-in-law's feelings. *Jathera* worship is common in some families. After the wedding, the bride has to worship the *jatheras* by *matha tekna* (bowing down) to a spot prepared by an elderly woman in the family.

In addition to worshipping saints and ancestors at local shrines, rural Sikhs also worship goddesses and nature. An integral part of Sikh sacred practices in the Punjab is the worship of the goddess *Devi*. She is worshipped under numerous names: *Durga, Kali, Kalika, Mahesri* and *Bhiwani*. She also manifests herself in the lesser deities *Sitala Devi, Mansa Devi* and *Naina Devi*. Major centres of *Devi* worship in Kangra, Hoshiarpur and Ambala in India attract thousands of Sikh and Hindu pilgrims at the annual and bi-annual fairs. Devotees often come to make a wish, or to give thanks after the fulfilment of a wish. Such wishes might concern the birth of a child, the success of a new venture, or the cure of an illness. One Sikh woman told me that, on the birth of her son, her mother-in-law instructed her to go to *Devi darshan* at Jwalaji (Madhya Pradesh).

Some Sikh families in England still go to Jwalaji for the *bhadan* (cutting of boy's original hair) ceremony. *Sitala Devi*, the Goddess of pustular diseases, is widely worshipped by Punjabi women, including Sikhs. This goddess was the eldest of seven sisters, a collective of disease goddesses, each responsible for inflicting and curing a particular disease. It is common in the Punjab to take a child to the *Sitala* temple to worship after the sores of a disease become dry. Many women still believe in taking children to the Hindu Temple for *matha tekna* (bowing the head in front of goddess) when a child has chickenpox. They also make sure that when someone in the family has chickenpox, onions, garlic, eggs and meat are not cooked in the house and *tarka* or *shaunk* (stir fry) are avoided. Since it is believed that *Sitala*'s wrath causes chickenpox epidemics, devotees hope to contain her anger by worshipping her.

Nature worship is also common in the Punjab. *Suraj* (sun) *Devta* and *Dharti Mata* (Mother Earth) are commonly worshipped. Brahmans are fed after each harvest to honour *Suraj Devta*. There are no shrines erected for *Suraj Devta* or Mother Earth; instead, a heap of stones or pottery is collected under the sacred tree of *pipal* (Ficus religiosa) or *barh* (Bengalensis) to mark a spot for the worship of Mother Earth. Rural folk go there to make offerings of milk, fruit and grain. It is also believed that a person who dies at the place where Mother Earth is worshipped attains peace. Because of this belief, when a person is about to die, he or she is removed from their bed and laid on the earth. Among the trees, *pipal* and *barh* are commonly venerated. Women worship *tulsi* (basil), which is considered a sacred plant. They water it in the morning and bow in front of it. Also part of nature worship is reverence for certain animals, among which the cow and bull are considered the most sacred. The cow is called *Gou Mata* (cow mother) and worshipped by all. Nature worship is not practised on the same scale in England. Cows are, however, considered to be sacred and many Sikh families do not eat beef out of respect for cows even though this is not forbidden by the Sikh religion.

Evil spirits, witchcraft, sorcery and magical healing

In popular demonology, evil spirits arise from the dead, especially if a death occurs under unfortunate circumstances. It is believed that a dead person's spirit wanders around as a *paret-ruh da bhatakna* (free roaming spirit) if the dead person has not been properly cremated. The spirit of the dead is transformed into a *bhut* (male evil spirit or ghost) or, in case of a female, into a *bhutni* or *churel*. It is believed to be a troublesome spirit, inflicting fever and other diseases on the possessed. *Bhuts* accomplish all their tasks by night and cast no shadows while moving, as they cannot set their feet upon the ground. This is why those who are transporting the ashes of the dead sleep on the ground to avoid them (a very common practice among Sikhs). The most dreaded *churel* is the spirit of a pregnant woman who dies during the festival of *Diwali*. It is presumed that *churels* entice men by assuming the form of beautiful women (*saledi*) and appearing at lonely spots to lure their victims. The only way they can be evaded is by paying no attention to their gestures or calls.

A person believed to be possessed consults the exorcist and acts on his advice. In complex cases, the exorcist sometimes lashes himself with a whip, and, in a paroxysm of dancing and head wagging, declares the name of the malignant influence, the manner in which it is to be appeased and the time when the disease may be expected to abate. Two exorcists were named in the survey.

Many of the methods and charms used by *sianas* (knowledgeable persons) are part of folk medicine. Charms are frequently used to cure minor ailments or improve flagging fortunes. For example, to cure piles a patient is asked to wind a thread of five colours (white, red, green, yellow and black) thrice around his thumb and at night the same thread should be transferred to the big toe. For the cure to be effective the thread should only be removed after a fortnight, on a Tuesday, the day sacred to the Hindu god *Hanuman*.

Some Sikh women believe that a powerful *siana* can cure a patient by his touch. This rite, which survives in the Punjab even today, is called *Jhara*, in which the *siana* will touch the afflicted part of a patient's body, mumbling a charm and touching the ground with a knife or broom at least seven times. Examples were given by women of using such methods in Birmingham and London. Religious Sikhs do not believe in *sianas* and regard them as fakes. They have begun to expose *sianas* and incidents have been highlighted by vernacular newspapers in the UK. One such incident was found in Leeds.

Despite this, there are Sikh women in England who believe and consult *sianas,* whom they believe to be capable of invoking divine powers. Such practices are fairly common in big cities like Bradford, Birmingham and London. At least three Sikh women in the survey admitted to using such sources to treat their illnesses and solve their problems. Another believed that her husband had been suffering from a mental illness, as his brother had fed him something given to him by a black magician. She went to a Muslim *pir* in Bradford, who gave her some water and asked her to remember the name of God. According to her, this person cured her husband. It is also common among rural Sikh women to worship healer saints, who often visit Britain. Recently a saint claiming to cure asthma and diabetes came from East Africa. The popularity of these people is confirmed by the advertisements of healers and astrologers in Punjabi newspapers in Britain.

It is obvious from this survey that Sikh women who came to England from the rural areas of the Punjab, and those from East Africa who originated in rural Punjab, believe in cultural values that are mainly Punjabi rather than Sikh. There is also a growing British-born Sikh population who may be somewhat influenced by their parents' views. However, the community has established *gurdwaras* and qualified *granthis* have been appointed. Most Sikhs attend the *gurdwaras* and have begun to devote more time to their religion, which has helped them to distinguish between Sikh beliefs and Punjabi culture. Consequently folk beliefs and traditions are gradually dying out. The younger generation interested in Sikh religious values also questions the validity of such practices.

Further Reading

Ballard, C. 'Arranged marriages in the British context'. *New Community*, 3, 1978, 181-196.

Ballard, C. Conflict, continuity and change: second generation South Asians. In Khan, V. S. (ed.). *Minority Families in Britain: Support and Stress.* London: Macmillan, 1979.

Ballard, R. 'Family organisation among the Sikhs in Britain'. In *New Community*, 2, 1973, 12-23.

Basham, A. L. (ed.) *A Cultural History of India.* Oxford: Clarendon Press, 1975.

Bhachu, P. *Twice Migrants: East African Sikh Settlers in Britain.* London: Tavistock, 1985.

Brah, A. 'South Asian teenagers in Southall: their perceptions of marriage, family and ethnic identity'. In *New Community*, 6 (3),1978, 197-206.

Chadney, J. G. *The Sikhs of Vancouver.* New York: AMS Press, 1984.

Dhanjal, B. ' Sikh women in Southall: some impressions' In *New Community,* 5 (1-2), 1976, 109-114.

Jyoti, S. K. *Marriage Practices of the Sikhs: A Study of Inter-generational Differences.* Delhi: Deep and Deep, 1983.

Kalra, S. S. *Daughters of Tradition.* Birmingham: Diana Balbir Publications, 1980.

Kinsley, D. *Hindu Goddesses: Visions of the Divine Feminine in the Hindu Religious Tradition.* Berkeley: University of California Press, 1986.

McMullen, C. O. *Religious Beliefs and Practices of the Sikhs in Rural Punjab.* London: Jaya Books. 1989.

Oberoi, H. *The Construction of Religious Boundaries: Culture, Identity and Diversity in the Sikh Traditions.* Delhi: Oxford University Press, 1994.

Shan, S. *In My Own Name: an Autobiography.* London: Women's Press, 1985.

Welty, P. T. *The Asians: Their Heritage and their Destiny. 3rd ed.* Philadelphia: J. B. Lippincot Company, 1963.

Wilson, A. *Finding a Voice: Asian Women in Britain.* London: Virago Press, 1978.

6

Listen to me

Women were interviewed for this report both individually and collectively. They offered insights into their own life experiences, good and bad. The stories they told were true and from the heart. They related their experiences, struggles, successes and disappointments. Many individual stories could have been written up but only a few have been chosen for inclusion here to illustrate the varied life experience of Sikh women. These stories relate not only to their achievements but also their struggles, reflecting the determination and desire of many women to succeed against the odds. These stories bring to life many of the issues for Sikh women that are discussed in the rest of the book. All names have been changed to protect their identities, and in some cases, some details have been slightly altered (but not the actual facts) to ensure anonymity.

Shalu (aged forty)

I belong to an educated and affluent family. My parents are from Jullundhur, in the Punjab. I was born in India and we moved to Kenya soon after my birth. I came to England in 1971 when I was ten years old. It was my parents' decision to migrate to Britain because of the Nationality Act. They would have lost their British citizenship if they had stayed in Kenya.

We always considered England as our mother country. The way English people lived in East Africa made us think that England was a prosperous country. Life there would be luxurious and prosperous. I was shocked when I came here to find white people doing menial jobs. The weather in England also shocked me, as the days were short and dark in winter, long and bright in summer. Zebra crossings were also something new for me.

I went to a primary school in Birmingham for one year. I did not have any language problems but I was sent to remedial classes. I found this utterly disgusting. Other black children were treated similarly. From there I moved to Middle School. I did not have any problem there even although the teaching methods were slightly different. After Middle School, I went to High School. Discipline in High School was not strict and there was a lot of freedom in the sixth form. I was tempted to enjoy that newly-found freedom and I started truanting. This went on for one term. After that, my parents came to know of my truancy and I was taken out of the school. I was not allowed to go out. I became bored sitting at home so my parents reluctantly allowed me to go out to work.

I got a job as a technician in a college. There was another Asian technician in my workplace. As it happened, we both lived in the same area and both took the same bus to work. We had a normal platonic work relationship, but community gossip was triggered by our sitting on the bus together. This is common when you live near other Asian families. Any interaction with the opposite sex is always interpreted as an affair. This gossip began to spread like wildfire and in the Sikh community losing one's *izzat* (respect) is the worst possible experience for a girl and her parents. I was only eighteen years old and my parents decided to marry me off quickly in order to save family prestige.

They arranged my marriage to a young man who lived near London. I liked the look of the boy they choose for me but I did not like his family. I told him that I wanted to live separately after my marriage, to which he agreed. He bought a house about half a mile away from his parents. Before my marriage, my in-laws somehow came to know of the gossip about my relationship with this colleague of mine. My father-in-law became furious and wanted to stop the marriage. However, pressure from his brothers and the suggestion of losing family prestige made him honour the marriage. Afterwards, I went to live with my in-laws outside London and away from my parents' home. They imposed all kinds of restrictions on me. I was not allowed to spend time with my husband. I could not sit with him and I was not allowed to go out with him. On family occasions, he used to accompany his parents without me. I was young and wanted to enjoy my life. I was imprisoned within the four walls of my married home and completely isolated. I asked for permission to work, which was refused by my father-in-law. My mother-in-law was working, so I used to cook and clean which were my allocated duties. I was not only young but also immature and adventurous. I wanted to look around this new town so I decided to go out and return home before they all came back from work. This became my regular routine.

After a few months of joint living, we decided to live separately in our own house. We painted and decorated it and I put all my dreams into this new home. We needed money for all of this so I started looking for a job. I worked with the Health Authority, the Community Relations Council and Social Services. Within this period of nearly six years, I matured and became fairly independent. We began to enjoy our life and socialised with my husband's friends.

There was always a conflict with my husband's family. They were critical of my behaviour, attitude and anything I did. They were critical of what I wore. According to them, I should not wear skirts, I should not attend evening meetings and I should not go to the pub for lunches with my work colleagues. I should not talk to or socialise with male colleagues. I tried to talk to them but it was of no use. Tension between us mounted. My husband, being the only son, was in the middle. His problem was that he never became mature and found it impossible to make decisions about his own life. He used to be wonderful when he was with me. When he was in his parents' company, he behaved like a child and his parents would make decisions for him.

The awful day came when my husband's family decided that he should divorce me. All kinds of allegations were made against me. I was accused of having a loose character, called a whore and a barren woman who could not produce children even after six years of marriage. I had not wanted to have children, as my married life was not stable. They took this as the inability to conceive a child. The whole idea behind this was to create a basis for divorce. They were quick to spread this around and more traditional women around me believed their lies, without making their own judgement. In a way, they were forcing me to leave home. I packed my clothes in a small suitcase (which was all my property at that time). My eyes filled with tears, as I repented of my decision to marry into a large joint family. My feet were moving to the front door when I saw my husband at the side of the door. I could not resist asking him what my fault had been. He took my suitcase and told me to stay, failing to find any fault in me. I obeyed him like a child and sat on the sofa.

I was sobbing, unsure of my future. My parents, who were unaware of the whole situation, were shocked to find what I was going through. They visited me and asked me what I wanted to do. I told them to wait and see. They decided to move near me in order to support me. My in-laws' despicable behaviour made me more determined to fight and stay, even though it changed my whole personality. I started getting panic attacks, began to drink in order to sleep and put on a lot of weight. I became cynical and could not trust anyone.

I believe in the Sikh religion and my upbringing as a Sikh has given me a lot of strength. This helped me to think through my situation. I realised that I had married into a family with very different values and beliefs to my own, and that I would have to become courageous and start living my own life in my own way under their roof. Eventually we bought a fabric shop, which began to make a good profit. My in-laws begged us to live with them again, to which my husband agreed against my wishes. They once more spoilt our life, which had just begun to run smoothly. At the same time, my husband started going out with another married woman who was working in our shop. He became seriously involved with her. In the beginning, it did not bother me, as I knew his flirtatious character. When I found that he was serious and was spending most of his evenings with her, I began to question him and took some steps to stop him. At that time, his parents were away on holiday in East Africa so I called his sister and his uncles, but it was no use. When his parents came back from their holidays, I told them. They did not seem to be concerned. Instead they started accusing me of failing to satisfy him. They indirectly supported his behaviour and his extra-marital affair. Things became so extreme that it was the talk of the town. Once again I was accused of being an uncaring wife who had failed to look after their son. This time, I refused to give in and became so strong that I not only faced up to them but also answered back in the same filthy language that was used towards me. I also started behaving in a manner that annoyed them. I used to please myself by coming and going from home at any time I felt like. I used to stay out late at night. The thought of separation crossed my mind several times.

One day I shut my eyes and gave serious thought to my future. I decided not to leave. The reason was that by this time I had three children. If I left him, I would have to take my children with me, as they were the only source of my strength. As a single mother, I would have had to struggle hard to bring them up. I was prepared to do that but I would not have been able to stop their father seeing them and having contact with them, which meant interaction with their grandparents. Knowing my husband's family, they would have convinced the children that I was in the wrong. If my children accepted what they said, I would lose everything and this would be my defeat. I decided to stay and take revenge on them. I was only waiting for the right moment. As time passed, we lost our business and once again, my family and I were blamed for fiddling the money. We had to leave those premises so we rented a house and my in-laws made their own arrangements. Life again became hard and tough. I had to take two jobs to feed my children and pay off the debts.

I did a Higher National Diploma in Chemistry while I was working at the college as a technician. In order to stay sane under the circumstances, I decided to study further so that I could remain focused. After two years' hard struggle, once again we bought our own house. I always feel that I have wasted 22 years of my youth. I have so many deep scars that will probably remain with me until my death. One regret I will always have is having to suffer at the hands of an illiterate and orthodox family who are still leading a 1950s village life. In orthodox families, educated women are seen as destructive and potentially immoral. However, I always remember the advice given by my educated friend, 'Wait and see, you will shine while they waste their life and sink in the ditch'.

I looked only to myself for help and support. I did not want to cry on the shoulders of my elderly parents, as that would upset them. Struggling alone with my husband's family, the pressure of my job and the social pressures had changed my personality and

I became infirm and weak. Even now, there is no appreciation for anything I do and I am tired of constant criticism, bickering and fault-finding by his family and relations. I pray to God and wait for the day when my in-laws' family will experience the same treatment that they have put me through.

Ruby (aged fifty)

I was born on 13 *Kartik* (27 October) in the afternoon, in a small village near Phagwarar in the Punjab. I was the eldest of seven children. It was hard to accept the birth of a girl in rural Punjab though my birth as a girl was not mourned. In my case, it was a coincidence that, at the time of my birth, my father suffered a mild attack linked with mental illness and this illness was taken as the effect of my birth as I was born on the 13th, in the month of *Kartik* and in the afternoon. All these factors were considered to be inauspicious, which made me an undesirable child.

Despite this, I received affection from my *nani* (maternal grand-ma) and I enjoyed a good upbringing from her with lots of fresh air and nutritious food living in the countryside. My mother and I went to stay in Chandigarh where my father was working as an accountant with the State government. He was in favour of education, irrespective of gender. I was admitted into a religious school and completed my high school and intermediate educa-tion by the time I was seventeen. My mother wanted me to marry, as the custom of the day was to marry girls at a young age. She was not keen to send me into higher education. She was also worried about my dowry, as I had three sisters. Her anxiety was understandable, but I wanted to study. This created tension in the family and one of my uncles took me away for a month to calm the situation down. It was a blessing in disguise for me. His next-door neighbours were refugees from Pakistan and the women used to knit hosiery at home in order to make their living. I liked this idea as it could make me financially indepen-dent. I used to slip away from his home to the neighbours when they were having their traditional afternoon nap. I learned the skill of knitting socks and ordered my own machine.

It caused a scene and havoc in my parents' home when the machine arrived. My mother was furious, saying that I was ruin-ing their *izzat* by doing that kind of menial work. She accused me of taking independent decisions without consulting them. I remained determined to work and study in spite of her critical behaviour and attitude. My father watched the whole situation but did not say anything, which was helpful for me. Through this work I became acquainted with an influential person who helped me gain admission to college to do a teacher-training course. After completing this course with distinction, I went away from home for six months to do another course which enabled me to get a job in a government school. Now I became financially independent and I started a degree course on a part-time basis. There was no peace at home. My mother used to get upset by the comments made by other people that she was not marrying me off as I was working and therefore bringing money for the family. Despite the tense situation, I graduated and completed my Bachelor in Education. With this qualification I got a job in a High School teaching English and Mathematics. I wanted to go abroad to study but my parents would not allow it.

My parents now started looking for a suitable match for me as I was nearly twenty-four years old. Eventually they found a young man who was already living abroad. It was purely an arranged marriage. We had not met and had no idea about each other's temperament or habits. An arranged marriage is a gamble from which you can not escape but you have to oblige your parents. I suppose they work simply because girls are trained to be adaptable and willing to compromise in any situation simply because of *izzat*. The first time I saw my husband, I was upset. He had a big beer belly and looked much older than me.

Indian traditions require a daughter to leave her parental home and go to live with her husband and his family after marriage. I left my parental home and, before coming to England, stayed with my husband's family for about three months. I was disgusted with the treatment I received from his family. I have no hesitation in relating some events that are still fresh in my mind after so many years. Indian marriage ceremonies are elaborate and tiresome for the bride and bridegroom. They certainly need some rest and quiet time when it is all finished. I arrived in my in-laws' home at dawn. Rather than asking me to rest or offering me a drink, I was questioned about the dowry and what I had brought with me. I told them that all that I brought was in the big suitcase and my clothes were in the small leather suitcase. I also showed them the jewellery that my parents had given me.

They checked everything, including what I was wearing, and commented that my parents had not given me enough. Then it came to the clothes for the mother-in-law and other relatives. They were what they expected, but my mother-in-law was not happy because my father-in-law received a gold ring and she did not receive any jewellery. I gave her the ring given to me on *muh dekhai* (something given to the bride at the time of lifting her veil) to keep her happy. It was unfair on their part, as they only gave me one set of gold jewellery, which they asked me to return the very next day. There were many other undesirable comments. One of my husband's sisters said that her brother should have received his weight in gold, as he was a 'catch' from England. Being orthodox and materialistic, they saw no value in my education. I felt very hurt by their comments, especially when I found that his brother had lied about my husband's qualifications. They spent most of their time gossiping, back-biting and undermining others. I hated every minute I spent with them. I was also disappointed, as I had nothing in common with them. I was an independent and self-made woman. My ideals and inspirations were far higher than their bickerings about dowry and gifts. The only solace I had was that I was not going to live with them permanently, so I suffered in silence for three months and tried to avoid any confrontation.

I left India to come to England. It was sad to leave my parents, relatives and friends to go to an unknown place having no one there except my husband, whom I had hardly got to know. However, I was pleased to get away from his family. In the Sixties, the impression of England was that it was a gold mine and anyone who had gone there would be rich. My husband had lived here for four years before he came back to India for marriage. He had sent most of the money he earned to his family. They took everything from him and gave him nothing. They even refused to buy us the tickets to go back to England. The reality was that we came to England in debt. My husband's friend in Leeds sent him the return tickets with borrowed money. It was a terrible situation. We were in debt and I was expecting my first child. I was trying to pay off our debts by saving every penny before my child was born but there were constant demands for money from his family. I was determined to pay off the borrowed money before the birth of my child, which I did.

Our life became more difficult when my husband's brother and sister came to Leeds. This sister was the one who was critical of my dowry. She was always demanding something or the other from us, which we could not afford at that time. This gave her further reason to criticise us. His brother stayed with us for three years and my husband never asked him to pay for anything. In addition, we spent money on his wedding. His brother was not appreciative of what my husband did for him but created lot of problems for us. His wife was a local girl and they used to undermine us in front of other relations. My husband's sister used to support them against us. They used to go around talking about us behind our backs. These women were totally illiterate and had nothing better to do but gossip. I was very lonely as there was no one in England from my parents' family. I tried to do everything for my husband's family but in return I received nothing but criticism and rejection. They never accepted me as a part of the family, as I was different and not one of them. I found my husband's family more of a hindrance than a support.

In a new strange land, I began my life again from scratch. I started applying for jobs but found that my Indian qualifications were not recognised. I was also rejected on the grounds that I did not have any experience in this country. My husband did not have enough money either to support me or to send me for further education, as there were always demands for large sums of money from his family. My husband did not want me to work in factories so we decided that I should study further. I started an interpreting job in order to fund my fees to improve my qualifications. It was very hard for me to combine study, a job and the care of a child. While I was struggling with all this, his family were spreading rumours that I was going to university to mess around. They did not want me to succeed.

On top of this I experienced a lot of racism and sexism at university. In 1968, I was denied admission at the reception window without anyone asking me about my qualifications. In 1972, I was asked by one of my tutors why I was studying when I had a husband and family. After a hard struggle I managed to enter into the teaching profession on a very low scale. I worked extremely hard and eventually got a senior position. I worked in reception classes funded by Urban Aid. These jobs were completely isolated from mainstream jobs and other staff would hardly mix with me. I still remember the words of a principal that he did not want to see these 'wogs'. There are innumerable incidents that I can remember. During this time I found that Sikh women, like any other black women, had to over-achieve to get respect from their employers. I remember that my first report on the South Asian communities and their culture astonished other teachers working in the school and for the first time they showed me some respect. It cannot be denied that institutional racism exists. The structures and policies are based on mono-culture, including the justice system. A 'divide and rule' policy is used in order to undermine black managers. Sikh women managers do not receive the same support as their white colleagues do from their managers. There is hardly any encouragement to do better or expand their mainstream experience and this diminishes their chances of promotion. Senior positions offered to black people often consist of working in isolation without staff and financial management responsibilities. Sikh women suffer discrimination in the workplace not only from white people, but also from other Asians in power, on grounds of religion and language. In one local authority I was offered a job because of my specialist skills and experience, but non-Indian Asian councillors objected. I do not think that there is any point pretending that there is no racism. It has become a part of many Asians' daily life and they try to live with it. Calling '*paki*' to any Asian is fairly common. Racial harassment in terms of spoiling a garden, throwing stones, breaking windows, annoying behaviour by neighbours are common.

In my career, I felt that I had a lot of potential that was not recognised and that I was exploited in my jobs. For my own satisfaction, I did a lot of other things where I could experience a sense of achievement, for example, teaching cookery. It was rewarding and fulfilling as through my cooking skills, I raised lot of money for different charities. I have three children who were given a good education. They live up to my expectations and have a very focused life. We spend a lot of time together and we are a very close family. My husband eventually realised that I had been standing with him through thick and thin. I worked hard for his family and he began to appreciate my efforts.

I have worked hard all my life and now the time has come to enjoy my life. My husband's family has never accepted me and are not going to accept me now, because of basic differences in our attitude and thinking. I tried to compromise with them, and helped them when they needed it, but I refused to bring myself to their level. My parental family and relatives respect me and I have earned a lot of respect from the Sikh community in Leeds. I have been living in Leeds for a long time and acquired many British values that have helped me to adjust and integrate in this community. I also retain my Sikh identity, values and culture, which I adore, and I am proud to be a Sikh. I am aware that there are problems with Sikh organisations and the management of *gurdwaras*, but this cannot devalue the religion. The uniqueness of the Sikh religion cannot be over-stated.

Ami (aged seventy-three)

I was born in Chandigarh in the Punjab. My father was a supervisor in the cycle factory in Ludhiana. I have five brothers and four sisters. I had a happy and caring childhood. My parents gave me an education and I did Matric in the days when education was not common for girls in our community. After my matriculation, my parents were keen to marry me off and they found an educated boy. I was married in 1945 at the age of eighteen. My husband was a qualified teacher and was working as a lecturer in Lucknow, where I moved after my marriage.

We had two children and then my husband decided to go abroad to study English literature. He gained admission to Leeds University and came to study for a PhD in English literature in 1951, six years after our marriage. I stayed behind with my children in my in-laws' house. My in-laws were very kind to me and they looked after me in his absence. I wanted to join him as I felt lonely and also I was scared that he might keep a *gori* (a white girl friend) here, a normal practice at that time. We kept in touch and I always wrote him encouraging letters and explained how I could help him while he was studying. So I came to join him in 1956.

My first impression of England was that the weather was wet and cold. After arriving, I felt very lonely because of life behind closed doors. I also felt very isolated as there were no relations and family of mine in this country. Gradually I began to settle down and got to know other Sikh families living in Leeds and Bradford, and also other students. I had another two children after coming to Leeds. I felt very strange when I had my children in this country. There was no one to care for me. Those were times when I desperately missed my family. My husband combined work and study, so he had very little time for us. I could not go out to work because of my young children.

Life was also hard for my husband. He had to work on top of studying in order to meet family expenses. Even under those circumstances, he had managed to complete his studies by 1962 and was about to get his degree, so it was a terrible shock to then learn that he had leukaemia and had only a few months to live. He died at the age of thirty-nine, leaving me with our four children. I was totally shattered and did not know what to do. After my husband's death, life became lonely, hard and tough. I had four children to bring up and I was not financially secure. I could not speak fluent English, even though I was a matriculate. This was the time when I missed my family most. There was no one to fall back on except one of my husband's friends, who really helped me. These circumstances changed my entire outlook on life. I had to become independent and make my own decisions.

I could not go out to work leaving my children unattended at home. I did not know about any benefits or any other help given by the state. I decided to stay at home and look after my children knowing that I needed money to raise them. I became so short of money that I felt that I had to do something. I was good at sewing so I started working from home, sewing Punjabi suits (*salwar* and *kameez*). This not only helped me financially but also brought me in contact with other women, breaking my isolation and loneliness. I became popular with Punjabi women because of my sewing skills. In those days, an old friend of my husband, who was a fabric retailer, suggested that I open a fabric shop. This was a good suggestion as women could buy material from my shop and if they wished I could sew their suits. So I made a space to put fabric in one of the rooms facing the main road. My husband's friend promised to supply me with fabric without advance payment. I agreed to his suggestion. My house was near the university, which was a good location as most Sikh families were either living or buying houses around that area at that time. He kept his promise and supplied the material and I used to pay him on a monthly basis. Though it was a small business, it kept me occupied and met my basic needs. I could earn just enough money to meet my family expenses. I must admit that it was a hard job to look after the children, and sew and sell fabric. I used to work long hours but I never ignored my children. My children always took priority over my business and I tried to spend the maximum time I could afford with them. I gave them a good education, so that they could have a good and dignified life. I tried to fulfil my husband's dream of educating our children. I never thought about myself.

I was really pleased with the success of my children's education. All of them went to university to study. When my eldest daughter became of marriageable age, I started looking for a suitable match for her. In those days, my daughter went on holiday and met her distant cousin with whom she fell in love. I did not agree with her choice but she was determined to marry him, so the marriage went ahead. He belonged to a good family and was a medical doctor. Soon after her marriage, she found that he drank heavily and gambled. She owned two properties that were sold within two years to pay off his gambling debts. The marriage did not last and ended in divorce.

I used to believe in arranged marriages, as long as some choice was given to children. Parents choose a partner from a compatible family, a family of their own standing and social status, so that the interaction can be harmonious. I do not think that this system can be maintained now, though it is important to select the right kind of family. Children do not want to listen to parents now and would rather make their own decisions. It is also difficult to keep your children under control as the culture and the law of this country are not compatible with our culture. Having had that kind of experience in our family shocked us and my second daughter chose her own partner and decided to marry a *gora* (white man). She is extremely happy and they have a good life. She cares for and looks after me. My third daughter has decided not to marry unless she finds a compatible match. My son had a love marriage with an Indian girl that ended in divorce as she had an extra-marital affair. He then married another Indian girl. She has no respect for me and hardly cares for our family. They make all kinds of excuses and pretexts not to look after me.

As I grew older, I decided to live on my own. I am a seventy-three-year-old lonely woman without any help and support. My children are scattered, living away from Leeds except for one daughter. Normally I can manage as I have been independent all my life. However, I feel completely lost when I am ill as there is no help from any of my children or from Social Services. Sometimes it makes me angry as I did so much for my children but got little in return, especially from my son. No one expects financial help from children in this country. Parents only expect love, respect and care from their children, especially from their sons. There are occasions when I strongly feel that I have lost my children in this western culture. Children are the main wealth of any parents. We came to this country to better our lives but many of us have ended up losing our real wealth – our children. I came here in the hope of an easy and luxurious life with high status but I have ended up with nothing.

The family is a source of strength for Sikh women. They do everything to further their families. I wanted to have a close family. In my case, my dreams were shattered and remained unfulfilled. My children lead their own life, according to their own ways. They do not want to listen to me. I always wanted to see harmony among my children, leading to a caring and warm relationship. They are, on the contrary, self-centred and not family-oriented. Now I do not have any expectations and want to live by the day, as it comes. It is strange that many of us are materially happy and lead a comfortable life after so many years of hard work, but there are few who are mentally contented. Our expectations are hardly met. We have worked hard, respected our elders and tried to be caring mothers and good housewives. We are not given the same love and respect by our children.

Dolly (aged sixty-two)
I come from a very disciplined family, as my father was a military officer. He did not allow my mother to work and used to say that caring for the family was a very responsible job. It was common in the Punjab at that time that the women were expected to stay at home to look after their own family and extended family. It was not considered honourable for a woman to work for a wage. I was brought up in a caring and loving environment. My mother was always with me when I needed her. She used to tell me stories before I went to bed. I was never short of anything. My parental home was very clean and tastefully decorated. I used to play outside the home in the open with my friends and in the home with my toys and dolls. My grandparents lived with us and

I used to go out with them walking, shopping and visiting their friends.

I was admitted to a school at the age of six. I liked going to school. I made a lot of friends and I became a favourite of my teachers, as I was a charming, bright little girl. I took an interest in my studies and sports. I became an outstanding student and passed all my examinations without failure. I passed my matriculation examination with high marks at the age of sixteen. My father encouraged me to study further and I did my FA (Intermediate exams) and Punjabi Honours. My parents started looking for a suitable husband for me as I was nineteen years old by then.

As it happened, they went to a wedding reception where they met a woman from Malaysia who had come with her son to find a wife. My parents met this boy. He was educated, handsome and had a good personality. They liked him and invited him and his mother for a meal. They both came to see me. I fell in love with him at first sight and he also liked me. His mother was impressed with our living standards, perhaps in the hope of getting a huge dowry. The date was fixed for the engagement ceremony. His mother wanted to do everything quickly so that they could return to Malaysia as soon as possible. The wedding arrangements were made and we were married within a month.

I went to live with my mother-in-law after the marriage. She had a big house in India with many rooms. However, we were not given a room for ourselves. The three of us used to sleep in one bedroom. She would not allow me to talk to my husband. They both used to go to see their relations, leaving me at home on my own. All the clothes and jewellery given by my parents were locked away and she had the key. I was only given two suits to wear.

They left India after three weeks, giving me the hope that I would be sent a ticket to join them as soon as they reached Malaysia. I went to stay with my parents after they left. I told my mother everything. Both my parents were annoyed and disappointed. My father asked me to divorce my husband. I could not think of taking that kind of action. It would be such a shame not only for me but also for my family and I would lose respect in the community.

Days passed, weeks passed and months passed. There was no communication either from my husband or from his family. After a year, my father advised me to study further as he did not like to see me sad. I did my teacher-training and got a job. My life became normal and my father advised me to remarry. While I was thinking seriously about this, I received a letter and sponsorship papers from my father-in-law, after four years. All of a sudden, everything changed. My parents did not want me to leave, but I said to them that I was a married woman and I should go. Eventually, after long discussions, they bought me a ticket and I left with a couple who were acquainted with my father. My father requested them to take me to my in-laws' house personally. He also wrote to my husband the date and time I was arriving in Malaysia.

When we arrived, there was no one to receive me. I was once again disappointed and got very worried. Soon after, I found out that there was a train ticket which had been left for me with the seaport authorities. The couple I went with did not like this and they wanted to accompany me to my in-laws' house. I said they should just put me on the train and not worry. They did so reluctantly. When I reached my destination, my husband and his mother were there to receive me. We went home and I found that there was no welcome. I got upset and worried, but by this time, I was determined to make things work. I was not given any food and I was told to sleep on the floor in my husband's room, which was shared by his younger brother. Both the brothers slept on the bed and I slept on the floor. I cried that night, feeling tired and hungry.

I was used as a cook and cleaner for the family. Once again, my mother-in-law took all my belongings and left me with only two suits. I used to wear one and wash the other. I was not allowed to iron my clothes and I was given leftover food. There were days when I had to go without food or was half-fed. My mother-in-law used to dress up and go out after having breakfast, leaving me behind to do the daily chores and other jobs like sewing and embroidery. She used to lock me in so that I could not talk to anyone. I was not allowed to serve a meal to my husband or offer him a drink when he returned from work. I was not even allowed to talk to him directly. He always left for the office before his mother. I never had a chance to see him alone. I was only allowed to go to the bedroom when both brothers were sleep. If his younger brother had to go away, his mother made his sister sleep with my husband. This went on for two years. My parents got worried when they received no letter from me. They wrote to some distant relatives, asking them to visit me. They came to see me. They said to my mother-in-law that they would like to talk to me alone. We went out and I cried and cried. I could not talk except to say that I was treated like a servant and there was no contact between my husband and myself. The three of us returned home and they asked my mother-in-law's permission to take me to their home. She did not like that. Then they talked to my husband and father-in-law. Eventually it was decided that I would go and stay with my husband as he was then working away from home.

I went with him. Our life became normal and we came to know each other. He was very scared of his mother. After two months, I became pregnant. My mother-in-law used to ring my husband every so often pretending she was seriously ill. He always visited her straightaway leaving me on my own. Then the day came when he told me to go to live with his mother so that she could care for me at the time of birth. I obeyed my husband and came back to stay with my mother-in-law. I found that nothing had changed. No rest was given to me, instead I was made to do everything in the house. One week, my mother-in-law went away with my husband leaving me with my brother-in-law. He was good and kind to me. When my husband came back, he accused his brother of having an affair with me. He kicked and punched him badly. As a result, his brother left home. Then the day came when I was blessed with a son. I was extremely happy but my happiness did not last for very long. After three months, they decided to send me back to India, keeping my son with them. I did not want to leave my son behind. They did not listen to me and put me on the ship to India. All the way back I cried. I was in pain as my breasts were full of milk. There was a couple with a baby in the cabin. They gave me their baby to hold when they came to know of my story.

I stayed in India for two sad and miserable years. My father, after retiring from the army, came to England and he brought me to Leeds with him. I started working in order to pass my time. One day, I gathered that my husband had also arrived in Leeds. He came to my father's home to take me with him. My father did not want me to go back with him but I was desperate to see my child. Just for my child, once again, I went with him. I was extremely happy to see and hold my baby though I did not have any feelings left for my husband and his family. I did not want to lose my son again and wanted to care and look after him. My parents stayed in Leeds to support and help me in settling down. Life once again became settled and I became pregnant and gave birth to a daughter. I was happy to care for my children and left my job to look after them. We bought our own house. This was the time when my mother-in-law arrived but luckily she did not come to Leeds but stayed with her younger son. After a year, my husband decided to move to London so that he could be nearer his family. I was reluctant but could not persuade him to stay in Leeds. We moved to London.

As soon as we moved to London, his mother wanted to come and stay with us. She looked miserable and desperate. My younger sister-in-law had thrown her out as she was playing the same silly games with her as she had done with me. My sister-in-law was a British-born girl and would not tolerate that kind of behaviour. One day, my mother-in-law slapped her. She called the police and reported the matter. The police came and asked my mother-in-law to leave her house. She had to quit and finding nowhere to stay, she came to stay with us. My mother-in-law now tried to be nice to me and began to work on a divide and rule strategy. She failed to succeed in this, as I knew her too well. I was only tolerating her in order to oblige my husband. I did not have any affection or respect for her. For me, only my children were important. I wanted to live for them and no one else. I learnt to cope with her and I am sure that she came to know that the law in this country would not approve of her behaviour.

My children grew up with a lot of love and care. I tried to meet all their needs. In return, they loved and respected me, unaware of what I had gone through. I did not tell them anything about the rough time given to me by his mother, as I wanted them to respect their father. After completing their schooling, they went to university. My son became an architect and my daughter became a teacher. They both got very good jobs. My son got married to an Indian girl and emigrated to Australia. My daughter chose her own husband, got married and moved to Scotland.

Now my responsibilities were over. There was and still is a rift between my husband and myself. I have no feelings for him and his family. We are living under one roof because of our marriage licence. He became ill and is a loner. I want to enjoy my life. I began to pursue my hobbies and started painting. I also joined women groups and associations. Now, I do not require permission from my husband, but only tell him where I am going and what time I will be coming back. I visit my children when I feel lonely and sad. Life goes on but the shadow of my past follows it closely.

Anu (aged thirty-five)

I was born in Mumbai in India. I was the third child in the family. I have two older brothers so my parents were thrilled to have me. I had a very happy upbringing. My childhood was spent in an extended family with my paternal uncles and aunts. There was always some one to talk to, to play with and to share things with. Grandparents often spoil (in a good way) grandchildren and this happened with me. My grandmother used to tell me stories and I used to go to the beach with my uncles and grandfather. The vivid memories of my childhood are still fresh in my mind. My father had a responsible government job and was a very busy man but I remember that we spent time with him, especially in the summer holidays. My mother was always busy doing or supervising household chores for the family.

The day came when my two uncles came to London. Later, they sponsored my grandparents and my auntie. The house became empty. I used to run around the house when I felt lonely. On occasions, I used to cry because I missed them. I was eight when my uncle wrote to my father to join them in London. I was excited and thrilled to hear that news. I wanted to be with them. We came to London when I was nine. My father was reluctant to leave his job, but family love made him resign.

After our arrival in London, we stayed in the big house bought by my uncles. Once again, we were together, laughing, joking and teasing each other. My father found it difficult to get a similar job in England, so he bought a grocery shop. Both my parents were liberal and fair and always consulted the family before making any final decision. My father had overall responsibility for the family, whereas my uncle kept an eye on the young ones. All the children were very scared of my uncle.

I started my schooling and began to settle in the school. I was good at my studies. My uncle kept a check on me, watching what time I came from school and where I went. After school, I used to help my father in the grocery shop, which gave me lot of confidence in dealing with people. I had a very protected life. I remember that I went to an Indian festival with my friend and on our way back the car broke down and I came home at midnight. My father was upset and my uncle was furious. I was also monitored for what I wore. Once, I wore a slit skirt at school and I remembered hiding that slit with my file so that my uncle should not see it.

Once we settled in this country, the first priority was to find wives for my uncles. My parents began to look for girls for them and they both got married. My auntie's marriage was also arranged. After her marriage she went to live with her in-laws. My other cousins also had arranged marriages. My father had a very close friend who lived in Liverpool. They had known each other from childhood and the friend wanted me to marry his son. We went to attend a wedding in Leicester and he also came with his family. Both families once again sat and talked about the good old days spent together. He also reminded my father of the promise made when I was born that he would make me his daughter-in-law. I was only fifteen then. My father replied that I was at school and wanted to study. Both families kept in touch and after a year when his son got a job in Leeds, he wanted to know my father's decision. We met a couple of times in a family environment. My father agreed to this marriage but suggested that I should complete my GCSEs. My mother consulted me and asked me if I wanted to marry him. I did not know any better and gave my approval. I still laugh to myself when I remember those moments. It was romantic, like Bollywood movies where two people meet at a wedding, like each other and marry.

I got married at the age of seventeen after completing my GCSEs. Six months passed. I went to live with my in-laws who by then had settled in Leeds with my husband. My mother-in-law was working and my sister-in-law and brothers-in-law were studying. I was also asked what I would like to do. I could not make up my mind and decided to stay at home. I used to cook, clean and look after the whole family. I soon got bored. I applied for a summer job and started working in a packing firm. It was a monotonous job and I decided to study instead. My mother-in-law was very pleased with my decision, as she wanted me to study and get an office job. I did some courses, which enabled me to do clerical and administration jobs. I worked for a year on a clerical scale in a college. I enjoyed my job and learnt a lot. After two years of marriage I was pressurised to have a child, which is normal in Asian families. I had a son and once again I became a housewife looking after my son and the whole family. It was not only tiring but also unrewarding. Everyone expected me to do everything for them, as I was at home all day. I decided to do a part-time job to escape from these domestic responsibilities. This job was the beginning of my career.

I impressed some senior people in the department I worked in. I was advised to study further and did some more courses related to my work. In between, I had my second child. This time, I kept my job. It was hard to look after two children, study, work and share other family responsibilities, since we were still living in the extended family. After five years, a full-time vacancy came up in the department and I applied for it. I got it and worked in this post for five years. I then felt ready to move on and I applied for and got a project manager's job. This job gave me many new experiences such as working with councillors and dealing with the media. By this time, my children had grown up and they could look after themselves. My brothers-in-law had also married and the house we had could no longer accommodate everyone. My husband and I bought our own house and started an independent life. My family responsibilities decreased and I had more time to spend on furthering my career.

There was a job advertised at senior management level, which seemed quite challenging and I was ready to accept this challenge. I had the qualifications and experience to apply for this job. I applied for the post and got it. I enjoy my work and I can also deliver. On some occasions however, I feel very lonely. At work, there is hardly any support network for black women. It is also difficult for some white people to accept a black manager and they feel uneasy and therefore create problems. I cannot discuss work-related problems at home with my husband, as we are not in the same field of work, and at times I feel that he may not realise the real extent of the pressures and responsibilities in my working life. I also have to maintain two cultures and constantly switch from one culture to another, which is not easy. I have to maintain my image and *izzat* in the community. In spite of all this, I take pride in my identity and in my achievements. I worked very hard to reach where I am. I was inspired and encouraged by my in-laws to study. Without their moral support I would not have followed this route. Sometimes we have bickering and disagreements, but one has to cope with this to remain in an extended family. I feel very lucky to be part of a family that has made me feel like one of them, and given me a sense of belonging not experienced by many Sikh women.

Komal (aged forty)

My parents originally came from Rawalpindi, a town now in Pakistan. After Partition in 1947, my grandparents crossed the border and came to Delhi where they were allotted refugee accommodation. During the move they lost their property, land and other belongings. My father and his family were lucky to cross the border safely. My grandfather tried to establish a business with his relatives as a joint venture in Delhi. It was not easy for him as he hardly knew anyone there and had no capital to invest. He worked very hard to make a living. My father started a degree in civil engineering, but as he was taking his final examination my grandfather had a massive heart attack and died. My father was shocked. He was left with business and family responsibilities, as he was the only son out of four children. The other business partners started fiddling money after my grandfather's death and eventually it was settled that they would keep the business, and some money was given to my father as settlement.

The man who was later to be my maternal grandfather was a friend of the family so he helped my father. He advised him to apply for government jobs and in the end my father got a good job. My grandmother was a shrewd woman and she married her two daughters with the money that came from the business. It became easy for my father to look after my grandmother and one sister. Over the next three years, my father managed to save enough to arrange the marriage of his youngest sister. My maternal grandfather had always liked my father and he married my father to his daughter. My mother was studying then. She was allowed to continue her studies and on the completion of her studies, she got a job.

I was born after five years. My mother kept her job and my maternal grandmother (*nani*) looked after me. I spent most of my time with my *nani* and was loved by my mother's younger sisters and brother very much, being the first grandchild in the family. My grandparents loved and spoiled me. My parents decided to move near my *nani* and they were very lucky to get accommodation nearby. By this time, I had become so attached to my grandparents that I did not want to come home, and stayed with them.

My parents were working hard to establish themselves. After three years my mother gave birth to my brother. During her pregnancy and after the birth of my brother, she stayed with my granny so that she could be cared for. I felt thrilled to see my baby brother. His skin was soft and I loved to touch him. My mother did not want to overburden my grandparents by leaving the responsibility of caring for both children, even though my granny offered. My mother decided to leave her job to look after us. I did not want to come to my mother. My grandmother suggested to my mother that she put me in a nursery so that I could learn to share and mix with other children. My grandfather used to collect me and then we would spend a few hours at my mother's house after the nursery. Time passed and I was old enough to go to school. My brother also grew and once again my mother thought of working. While she was exploring these possibilities, my father got another well-paid government job. Eventually it was decided that my mother would not work.

I went to a local school where I did my Higher Secondary and later went to university to do a BSc. I then decided to attend a teacher-training course for which I had to move away from home for a year. After completing my training, I was lucky enough to get a job in a secondary school as a science teacher, teaching chemistry. This gave me an incentive to study further and I did a Masters in Science. By doing this degree, I got promotion and became a postgraduate teacher. I was very happy in my teaching career as it offered me a wide variety of experience. For the first time I learnt to use a computer and I became so interested that the school sent me on many computer courses.

My parents now began to insist that I marry. I did not want to marry as the 1984 Hindu-Sikh riots in India had disturbed the Sikh community very much. I wanted to dedicate my life to the women and children who lost everything in these riots. I started voluntary community work and taught in the camps opened for them. This gave me the motivation to open an academy for teaching science and computing. I also did some consultancy work in information technology. At this time, my mother became seriously ill and there was hardly any chance of her recovery. My mother once again tried to persuade me to get married. I promised her that I would do so as soon as she recovered.

Miraculously, my mother did recover and my parents started looking for a husband for me. They started looking at matrimonial columns in journals, a common practice now followed to arrange marriages. They saw an advertisement in a national paper from a man living in the UK. They started negotiating. After a month, he came to Delhi and we spent a month courting in order to know each other. I liked him, though my parents somehow were not keen on him. However, they respected my wishes reluctantly. The marriage was arranged and the wedding was performed.

In the first week after the marriage, I came to know that he was a divorced man, a fact he had not previously disclosed. I could have accepted this, but the mess he was in seemed terrible as there were still disputes going on from his divorce. In spite of all this, I accepted him and told him that he should settle everything as soon as possible so that we could start afresh. In order to ensure that everything was in order, I insisted that he register our marriage and apply for a visa for me.

He stayed with me for three months in India. We travelled around and I found that he changed after the wedding. He used to swear and use filthy language if he could not get his way, showing no concern about my feelings. I was unsure of what to do. After he left for England, I got my visa. I was reluctant to join him as I was tense and fearful of his behaviour and my parents were fully supportive of me. The time came for the visa to run out and I had to decide one way or the other. It was eventually decided that I would go. I came to Leeds and had an initially enjoyable few days.

Soon after, life started taking another turn. Every move of mine was watched and I was criticised even for small things such as the way I cleaned and cooked. I took all the criticisms in a positive manner, thinking that it was a settling-in period. I was not given any money and did not have any say whatsoever in any matter. I was insulted on most occasions and threatened that I would be sent back if I did not obey his orders. I was under enormous pressure to find a job, it did not matter what. I was told that he had huge financial debts and that I should work to bring in money.

I found contract work for six months in the university as a research technician. I had to adapt to the new working conditions in a different culture and environment. Part of my job was to take groups of students around the laboratory for demonstrations and that was nerve-wracking for me in the beginning. At home there was constant pressure, bickering and criticism. I was even asked to borrow money from my relations living abroad in Singapore and Australia. My husband also asked me to sign papers in order to raise loans in my name, about which I was hesitant and refused to sign. He could not accept this refusal and threatened to deport me. I remained calm and did not let him have his way. It became a routine matter for him to swear at me and on occasions violence took place when he was angry. I was forced to have sex when I was tired and sleepy. This whole situation drained me completely, both mentally and physically.

On our first wedding anniversary we had a serious confrontation. In his anger he kicked me after a heated argument. After this, I was punished severely if I cried or looked sad. I tolerated all this in the hope that I could change him to make my marriage work. On the night of *Diwali*, the Indian festival of lights, we had an argument when he wanted me to sign some documents and I refused. He lost his temper and swore at me using filthy language. I was beaten up badly and bruised. My mother and other relatives rang to wish me a happy *Diwali*, as it was our first *Diwali* after my marriage. I was so stressed that I could hardly talk. My mother rang a friend of hers and asked her to visit me and see if I was all right. She came with presents and saw my bruises and understood everything. She rang the police when she went home and the police came. They took me to the nearby police station when they saw my bruises. They interviewed me, advised me to take legal action, brought me home to pick some essential belongings and escorted me to a refuge where I spent my night crying and sobbing thinking about my future. For me, it was a temporary measure so that the situation could calm down and my husband could have time to think. On the contrary, however, it made him more determined to deport me back to India.

My new life started in the refuge where the staff gave me support and good advice at a time when I was desperate and lonely. They were very helpful. I had people around me twenty-four hours a day. The only thing I disliked there was the food, as I had not become accustomed to British food. I had two major problems to solve. My first problem was harassment from my husband, for which they advised me to take an injunction from the court and I did that. The refuge workers got me legal aid. The second problem was my immigrant status. The workers gave me good advice, which I followed and I got permanent residence in England. Now I was in a strong position to fight my case. My husband was shocked to hear that I had permanent residence and would be fighting my divorce case in this country. I fought my case as strongly as possible, but it took me two years to get a divorce.

It was a miserable time for me. I had no friends and relatives to support me either morally or financially. I was on my own in a strange land. I didn't like to travel on my own. The only support I had was my mobile phone, which connected me with my loved ones. My family in India gave me lot of strength and support. This whole situation put me under a lot of pressure and stress resulting in depression. I became very weak, lonely, isolated and lost interest in my own life. There was no Indian organisation or network to support women in distress. I used to gaze at the bare and dirty four walls of my council flat for hours. Eventually I began to feel that I wanted to start my life afresh. My first priority was to get back my strength and health. I feel fine now and am settling in this country. I am concentrating on my career and want to get a job in order to be able to buy my own house so that I can have a fresh start.

I am fully aware that it is not an easy task to start again as there is a stigma attached to divorce. It is difficult for a single woman to have a full social life and remarry. It is also the experience of many single women that some men take advantage of them and make advances towards them. However, I am sure that the support from my loved ones and my own determination will help me in making my future life happy and successful.

Nindi (aged thirty-five)

I was born in a big village near Phagwara in the Doaba region of the Punjab. I was the youngest of five children. I have only one brother, who is one year older than me. We quarrelled as much as we played and had lots of fun together; at the same time there was an element of rivalry, animosity and finding ways to prove who was best. There was no doubt that at that time I felt that I was much more intelligent and active than my brother, willing to do things and participate in sports. I was quite tomboyish. I was bold, confident and not hesitant about fighting back to defend myself against physical or any other attacks. I never liked to give in and be submissive even though I was brought up in a very traditional family. My upbringing was influenced not only by Sikh religious teachings but also by my father. To me he was 'Mount Everest', strong, confident and always ready for a challenge. Nobody dared confront or challenge him, except myself because I knew I was his favourite. To this day I see him as my role model, to whom I looked up. I learnt Punjabi and was the first girl to sing hymns (*gurbani*) in the temple, a hall that we rented every week.

We came to England when I was five, to join my father in Leicester. My father bought a big house before our arrival. It was furnished with all the facilities of hot water, inside toilet and carpets, but I hated the life behind closed doors. There was no one to play with me and I could hardly go out to play because of the weather. Even to this day I do not like the cold weather. Once I started school, things changed for me. I began to enjoy my life. It took me some time to converse fluently in English, and at the time I could not understand why other children laughed. This did not prevent me from making lot of friends when I settled in my school. Being the only boy, my brother always got preferential treatment and from a young age I felt the need to show that I was more intelligent. I remember an incident when my father asked us both how big was an inch. My brother opened his arms wide to show an inch and I indicated with my thumb and big finger the width of an inch. My father walked to my brother and slapped him but I felt the pain. At the time I felt very guilty for giving the right answer but at the same time felt a great sense of achievement, and I knew that I had made an impression on my dad.

I used to come in the top three in any class test but I was also highly talented in sports. I took part in local and regional events such as hockey, netball and tennis. Art was my favourite subject. I had ambitions to be a radiographer, but teachers in the 1970s always encouraged black people to study art or sports, hence the reason I studied for a Diploma in Art. I did not realise at that time why most of my black friends had gone to college to study art or sports or instead went straight into employment. None of us were encouraged or supported, and we had to be grateful for what we had. I was in my late twenties when I found out what racism and other 'isms' actually meant. Looking back I feel cheated and let down by the education system of the seventies and eighties and I'm sure the young generation of today will have something to say about racism in education. The difference between education today and back in the seventies was that none of us black people then knew or understood the term 'racism'. All we knew was that we were a different colour and that was that.

Whilst the majority of white people were given the opportunity to sit 'O' levels, Asian and black people had no choice, they had to do CSEs (Certificate of Secondary Education). Because I was very good at tennis I dreamt of playing at Wimbledon, but my dream was shattered when my dad said, 'Asian girls don't do that sort of thing'. So as well as being deprived of academic study at school, I was also told I could not continue tennis. Looking back, I realise that like many other Asian women of my time, I lived to please other people, not myself. However, not only am I now a new woman, but a new Asian woman in my own right.

My results for my Art Diploma were excellent and my teacher came to our house to persuade my father to send me to university, to do textile design. Somehow I just knew that this was a bad idea. My father's views and aspirations were totally different; he wanted me married off, as my other three sisters were married by the time they were nineteen and I was then eighteen. My father stood like Mount Everest with his arms firmly folded, leaning against the fireplace. He told my teacher, who was also my friend, that, 'none of his daughters went to university but they could do whatever they wanted after they got married in their own (matrimonial) home.' To this day I remember her trembling voice saying, 'What are you going to do if she comes back?' 'That doesn't happen in our culture!' my dad replied. Little did he know at the time, that I would be back in eighteen months for good, and as a mother.

Within a year, my parents found a husband for me in Derby and we had a traditional Sikh wedding. I went to live with my in-laws in Derby, but they did not want me to work so I stayed at home. The grandmother visited me every other day like Miss Marple to investigate what I was up to. My day started at six in the morning, making breakfast for the family, cleaning the house, washing and ironing clothes, preparing the lunch and then I had an hour for myself before preparing the evening meal. This was my daily routine. I was not allowed to go out on my own. My mother-in-law used to work from Monday to Friday, and had headaches that miraculously started on Friday nights and ended on Sunday evening. She began to resent even the spare hour that I had, so she started piling up work for me to do, such as picking stones from amongst sesame seeds and sewing. I also gave in to pressure to have a baby and after two months of marriage I fell pregnant. I had severe complications in my pregnancy and my son was born two months prematurely, weighing just three pounds. My son was the only thing that kept me going. I thought that my life might change but it did not and my life became miserable and unbearable.

All the pressure and negativity towards me made me ill and I began to lose weight. My parents came to see my son and, finding me in that state, became very concerned. They asked the permission of my in-laws to take me away with them. I went to stay with my parents for one month. I regained the rosiness in my cheeks and my health began to improve. I told my parents everything and they were very angry. My husband came to collect me and my dad questioned him. When we got back to Derby I was banned from receiving or making calls to my family. My only means of communication with my family was by sending letters through the health visitor. One day, my husband and I were told to leave the house and we went to live on our own. I began to live my life the way I wanted. This did not last long as my mother-in-law and her mother kept their eyes on us. They used to tell tales to my husband and slowly he became aggressive and tried to be violent towards me. One thing my dad had taught me was never to allow yourself to be physically abused by your husband. Consequently, my husband resorted to throwing things against the wall. I used to be scared in case he hit my son or me.

One day I gave him an ultimatum that should he continue with this aggressive behaviour, I would leave, and this is exactly what I did. I picked up my son and ran and ran and ran. I was so afraid that I hid myself behind some bushes scared that he would find me. He looked around, I could see his head turning from side to side like a hawk hunting for prey. Luckily, the bus stop was next to the bush where I was hiding. I was in a dilemma because I could see the bus approaching. If I came out he would see me, but if I didn't get out to stop the bus I would miss it and he would find me anyway. My opportunity came when he gave up and was walking back towards the house and I popped out my hand to stop the bus. My heart raced as I saw him running towards me, but by then I was on the bus. I begged the driver to shut the doors and drive off. Looking back, it was like something out of a Hollywood movie. I had a friend in the town who owned a shop; I told her everything and she contacted my parents. My dad and my brother came to fetch me later that day and I never went back to Derby.

After eighteen months of marriage I came back to my parents with a glazed look from the awful things that had happened to me. I had been chased by my father-in-law with a knife, locked in my bedroom and had received continuous daily torment from my in-laws. How I survived, I still do not know to this day. I slowly pulled myself together and enrolled for night classes at college, because being at home with my sister-in-law had its own problems. How I longed to be on a desert island with my son.

I started living with my parents and applied for legal separation. My father regretted his decision to marry me so soon and tried to rectify this by supporting me in any ventures I did. I started working in order to finance my son and myself. My sister-in-law did not like my presence in my parents' house, as she saw me as a burden on them. She started discriminating against my son and expected me to share cooking and cleaning, even though I was out of the house for most of the day working full-time and studying in the evenings. I got so fed up that whilst my parents were visiting India I left their home and went to stay with my cousin.

With the help of my parents, I completed my degree and got a good job. Life once again became normal. My family insisted that I should remarry and settle down rather than running around from place to place. My father arranged for me to meet some young men. I made it very clear to my father that I would like to get to know any man who wanted to marry me before I committed myself again. I remember that my father introduced me to a man who was very rich and insisted that I give serious consideration to marriage. He was keen to marry me, but not interested in my son. Little did that man know that my son was my life and soul. Whilst visiting my sister I met my current husband; he got on well with my son, and my son liked him. We got married.

There is an Indian proverb that 'where there is more than one pan, they will always rattle'. Some members of this new family thought that they would be able to dominate and suppress me, simply because I was previously divorced. I think they expected me to be dumb or illiterate, but their expectations were wrong. I succeeded in every aspect, whether it was cooking, dress-making, education or simply life experience and best of all my husband is very supportive about everything I do. Eventually, the family had to give in and accept this, though they did not like it. I have settled very well in Leeds. I have a good job and I have had another son from this marriage. My relationship with my husband is more as if we are best friends; both of us are very happy.

My life has been, and to some extent still is, a chain of struggle and hardship, but each time I face a new challenge, I become a stronger person. If we 'professional Asian women' are fighting for our freedom or basic human rights at home, our employment is regarded as a form of escapism. If we are seen to be fighting for equality at work, we are regarded as feminists or as threats to the general workforce, which has problems of its own such as discrimination, sexual harassment or lack of promotion. Because Asian women are supposed to be 'timid Asian flowers', we are expected to do as we are told, while other Black women are seen as 'black mamas'; aggressive and not to be messed around with. Some unfortunate souls like me are cursed with struggles at work and at home, but we continue to try to balance ourselves on a double-edged sword.

7

Conclusion

Sikh women constitute a small proportion of the total Indian population in England. Women immigrants first arrived in England in the late 1940s. That number rose rapidly with the arrival of East African Sikhs from Kenya, Uganda and Tanzania in the 1960s and 1970s and with increasing numbers of Sikhs arriving from the Punjab. There are also a few Sikhs who came from Malaysia and Singapore. Early immigrants from India planned to work in England to earn money and then return home, but those plans changed when their wives and families joined them in the UK and they began to establish themselves, buying property and setting up businesses. East African Sikhs from the very beginning made England their home.

Sikhs living abroad have a strong sense of community, based on their adherence to the Sikh religion, to Punjabi culture and to speaking Punjabi amongst family and friends. Many Sikh women have integrated well into British society, adapting their life styles to combine Sikh and Punjabi beliefs and traditions with the British way of life. The second and third generation are re-adapting their culture and tradition to fit with the norms and values pertaining in Britain. A distinctive British Sikh identity is emerging which draws from the various influences, both traditional and contemporary, that shape Sikh lives here today.

The women in general have adapted well and accommodated to both cultures. They have retained the traditional ceremonies which help them to create an identity and maintain a high degree of cohesiveness. For example, the three ceremonies that accompany naming, marriage, and death closely follow the traditional pattern. A child receives its initial Sikh identity through its name; the name functions to link the child to its patrilineage and to the Sikh religion. An individual reinforces that identity at the time of marriage and the community reaffirms that same identity at the time of death. Marriage is probably the most important life cycle ceremony for an individual and it maintains the essential Sikh identity of the community. It may be inferred from this that the wedding ceremony itself, and marriage in general, mark a very important transition – a transition that is the concern of, and is monitored by, the Sikh community. However, religious practices that emphasise outward Sikh identity, for example, initiation, are becoming less significant. Initiation requires one to keep the five 'K' symbols of Sikhism, which differentiate Sikhs from the indigenous community but, nowadays, younger Sikh women trim or cut their hair and generally do not display the outward signs of Sikhism. This enables them to integrate within British society and be accepted more easily by other British people. Sikhs have opted for a compromise by keeping some ethnic traits, which maintain Sikh identity, such as traditional food, clothing, family values and family unity, festivals and ceremonies. This dual identity places greater emphasis on individual choice, while retaining a sense of duty and respect for the family.

This process can be seen in the field of education, with formal British education adding to the westernisation of Sikhs, while informal Punjabi language classes maintain a high degree of Punjabi identity. Other examples of how the community has reinforced separate identities could be taken from social and religious arenas. The growth of *gurdwara*-related activities supported by the Sikh community and the role played by social and cultural associations contributes to a distinct Sikh identity. The popularity of Indian food and fashion is another such example. Many Punjabi recipes and clothes are adapted to suit Western tastes and, conversely, many Western dishes and designs are modified to suit Punjabi tastes. As the Sikh community develops, it not only reinforces some of the original aspects of its identity but also reacts to the wider society and continually redefines itself.

As Sikhs have established themselves in the UK, they have grown more affluent. The increased earning power of women, in particular, means that they have a greater independence than their mothers and grandmothers ever had. Combining work and home duties leaves them with little spare time and consequently this is to some extent loosening kinship obligations. However, it should be stressed that the family unit is still very strong amongst Sikhs and the concept of maintaining family *izzat* and their own high standards is still central to how Sikh women conduct their lives. It is believed by Sikh women that '*izzat* once lost can never be regained'. Many Sikh women still sacrifice their own interests for the sake of family respect.

The family is central to Sikh women and their life revolves around their own or their extended family. Sikh women generally prefer to live in joint or extended families, either under one roof or in close proximity to one another. Compatible families share a common kitchen or live nearby, sharing childcare and spending much of their time together. Sikh families prefer to look after their children themselves or in the family environment; leaving their children in outside childcare is a last option. Sikhs try to maintain family relations even when they do not get along with each other – one reason why almost all families get together in times of crisis or celebration. The system works well generally, but women in the survey raised three main problems with joint living: lack of privacy, unwelcome interference from in-laws and criticism (*toka taki*). There seem to be greater problems for women who are working in professional occupations and who live in families where their relatives do not have a similar lifestyle. Some suffer stress and problems relating to incompatibility, spending too much time dealing with disagreements over petty differences, and they think their relatives do not understand their obligations and interests outside the family. Professional women often tend to move to more affluent areas, sometimes away from their families, to avoid conflicts and just maintain a civil family relationship.

The thinking of younger Sikh women on family relations also differs. For younger people, there are increasing bonds within their own generation, while the bond between the generations has declined. Young British-born Sikh women concentrate on their immediate family rather than the extended family and so the extension of the family unit is gradually losing its hold. The attitude of older Sikh women is also changing from a traditional one to a more accommodating one. They have come to terms with the fact that they cannot impose their decisions on their children. Their willingness to compromise with their children and accept changes reflects their flexibility. Families who are able to keep Indian values and traditions are happy, whereas those whose children have moved away from traditional values seem to be less content.

The vast majority of women still enter arranged marriages, although they now have much more say in their future marriage partner. Some women choose their own partner, with whom their parents are usually happy, as long as the man is a Sikh from their own caste. Other women have a partner chosen for them and are consulted before a final decision is made. It is very rare now for women to have no say at all in the choice of their prospective husband, as parents are much more flexible about the arrangements made for their daughters than in the past. However, parental support has always been a factor in the success of arranged marriages, and Sikh women are still keen to retain the support of their families. Sharan-jeet Shan in her autobiography, *In My Own Name*, commented on arranged marriages: 'When a marriage is arranged with the complete consent of both parties and a thorough appraisal of each other's backgrounds, it stands a very good chance of survival, maybe even a better chance than love marriages' (1985:ix).

However, there is a strong dislike of marriages outside caste and religion, and part of the reason that parents are becoming more flexible in their daughters' marriage arrangements is to prevent these unions taking place. Women are at risk of being ostracised from their family and community if they marry outside the Sikh religion and culture, although such marriages have been taking place ever since of Sikhs settled in the UK and are gradually increasing among younger Sikhs, despite parental disapproval and community pressure. However, these marriages seem to be proving generally successful, even without parental support. The future trend looks likely to be towards personal choice with the seal of approval from parents.

Though the caste system is repudiated by the Sikh religion, it does play an important role in marriage arrangements. One of the most important elements of an arranged marriage is that it should be within the caste. However, as inter-caste marriages increase, it seems that religion is gradually replacing caste in terms of finding a marriage partner and this is further restricting the expansion of caste-based bonds of extended family. The changing trend is further indicated in the choice of partners between upper and lower classes.

The selection criteria are also being affected. For first generation migrants, partners were selected on the basis of their character, economic independence, family status, physical appearance and age. The younger generation looks for compatibility, education, earning potential, intelligence, physical charm and moral values in their potential partner. The practice of importing brides and bridegrooms from the Punjab played a vital role in maintaining linkage with India and reinforcing the traditional family values but this practice has become less common with the expansion of the local Sikh community and the availability of eligible men and women. Young Sikh women generally want to marry British-born Sikh men, though there are some rare instances of importing a bridegroom from the Punjab. Education also seems to have affected the age at which people marry. It is a general trend for educated and professional Sikh women to marry later. The age difference between spouses has narrowed and the ideal gap now is one or two years.

The dowry remains a prominent part of arranged marriages (see Jhutti, 1998). Sikhs do not necessarily ask for one, but there is still a strong tradition in the community of expecting a dowry. The expansion of the dowry system in the UK is mainly due to the increased earning power of young women. A dowry can certainly help women set up their own home, but it restricts the education of some, as they have to sacrifice their education to work for two or three years in order to earn their dowry to conform to social conventions. Most women in the survey favour the dowry system, but a few commented that it was unfair. They felt that if both partners are economically independent and educated, it is wrong that a woman has to provide a dowry in order to be able to get married.

Most Sikh women take pride in their identity, religious and cultural values. Many are active within their local *gurdwaras*. *Gurdwaras* are central to their lifecycle rites and contribute significantly to their religious and social life. They take part in preparing and serving *langar* (the communal meal), and some teach Punjabi or music, while others are involved in *kirtan* (hymn singing). However, the management committees of the *gurdwaras* rarely reflect the contribution of women, being male-dominated and often controlled by particular families. Committees are often beset by infighting and by accusations of incompetence or malpractice. Women who did participate on management committees felt that their contributions were generally belittled and that they themselves were humiliated at times. Women have set up *istri satsang* groups (women's hymn-singing groups) in *gurdwaras* to meet their religious and social needs. It often happens that the wives and relatives of the members of the executive committees of *gurdwaras* dominate these groups, thus replicating *gurdwara* politics. There is therefore little involvement from women in the more prestigious and powerful areas of life within the Sikh community, despite the value placed on equality by the Sikh *gurus*.

Although the community appears on the outside to be unified, there are various divisions within it, based on class, caste and breakaway religious sects. Despite Sikh teachings, the caste system is deeply ingrained among Sikhs and it has often divided the UK community. Caste distinction does not normally operate in the day-to-day life of Sikhs but it has a marked effect on their marriages and their social relationships, making caste an integral part of Sikh life. There are caste-based and sect-based *gurdwaras* in England, and Sikhs have a strong allegiance to their caste and sect. For Sikhs, the class system is a newly emerging phenomenon in England, which further divides the Sikh community into wage earners, businessmen and professionals. Sikhs are also divided on the basis of their origin, that is whether they are Indian or East African.

Certain Punjabi traditions inform some Sikh women's lives, such as fasting, pilgrimage, black magic, *sharadh*, *jatheras* and consulting astrologers to determine auspicious occasions. Many Sikh women worship gods, goddesses, Hindu deities, local holy men and believe in superstitions. Older women in particular retain many such values. This results in multiple forces informing the Sikh community in this country: Sikh religious beliefs on the one hand and Punjabi traditions on the other. These various forces have become so intertwined that it has become difficult to un-ravel one set of values from the other. From time to time, Sikh revival movements appear which rely on a very strict morality, condemning outside influences, and try to revive the Sikh reli-gion in its original state of purity. However, these revival move-ments tend to become separate from mainstream Sikhism, rather than integral to it.

The Sikh women who first came to the UK began to work out-side the home fairly rapidly. They usually took menial or sewing jobs in factories, especially textile companies, and later some began to open small businesses of their own. Second and third generation women have a more diverse range of occupations. Many enter higher and further education and go on to pursue professional careers, combining work and family life. Many are now continuing their jobs, rather than giving them up to raise families. Professional women say that it is quite a strain to live what is essentially a dual cultural life, between work and home. At work they have to fit into British culture, while at home they follow Indian norms and values. Switching constantly between the two can cause enormous stress and confusion, especially if the women live in traditional households where the difference is more marked. Sikh women also experience racism and stereotyp-ing at work and often find it hard to socialise with work col-leagues after work. This further marks them out as different in some way. Some Sikh women I spoke to thought that race aware-ness training did not bring real change in the attitude of racist colleagues. Instead, it strengthened their racism by teaching them how to appear to be politically correct whilst maintaining their racist beliefs. There are not the same support networks for professional Sikh women as there are for white women and this can frustrate and demoralise women who need understanding and support for the work-related pressures they are often under.

Increasing awareness in Sikh women has made them realise that they are equal to men. Younger Sikh women have begun to ques-tion the duality in Punjabi traditions, one for a man and another for a woman. There are certain cultural norms which are ex-pected to be strictly followed by women and by which the be-haviour and character of a woman is judged and appraised by the Sikh community. This may not necessarily be applicable to men. Platonic friendships between the sexes are often frowned upon within the Sikh community, as it is not considered respectful to mix with the opposite sex, even after divorce. Men do not seem to have to put up with such restrictions. Young women now like to lead their life the way they want rather than the way Sikh society imposes upon them.

Social life for Sikhs has become rich in England, as they can take advantage of the facilities offered to both cultures. They can enjoy movies and concerts in English, Punjabi and Hindi. They eat out and go on holiday. Social functions in the Sikh community, such as birthdays and weddings, are elaborate and ostentatious. Sikhs now celebrate seasonal, religious and social functions on a large scale by having live entertainment and elaborate festivities reflecting Punjabi hospitality. Local social and cultural associations bring Sikh families together and play a significant role in keeping the traditional values alive. This gives them the opportunity to wear their traditional dress and enjoy Indian cuisine. As a result the variety and designs of traditional dress have increased and the traditional food has been generally enriched as a result of the cultural fusion and the availability and affordability of a huge variety of ingredients.

Although Sikh women have generally adapted well to life in England, various issues have arisen from integration into British life which has caused problems for the community. Isolation may be a problem for some Sikh women because of language and cultural barriers, the generation gap, divorce or lack of parental support (especially for women coming from India for marriage and women in mixed marriages). Elderly women find it difficult to access the support system set up for older British people, because of problems of language or culture. There is little support within the wider Sikh community, as it is expected that families will look after their own elderly members. Women have set up *kirtan* sessions amongst themselves and there are day centres for elderly Asians run by Social Services, but some expressed a wish to be able to follow a wider range of activities than the religious-based pursuits they follow at present. There are few suitable arrangements for active older women. The community ignores women who are divorced or separated from their husbands, because they have brought shame upon their families. Other women who do not have parental family in this country find that they receive little or no support from their in-laws, especially if they are having problems in their marriage.

Divorce has become more common in the Sikh community, as women have become more educated and financially independent and are no longer prepared to tolerate unreasonable behaviour from their partners or in-laws. Previously social pressure was exerted and a reconciliation process would be put into operation involving family and friends. Matters were not taken to court. The situation has changed now and marital disputes are settled in the courts, according to British law, which does not always accommodate ethnic cultural norms and values. Many Sikh women still stay in unhappy marriages and live in a permanent state of resignation, always compromising and making sacrifices for the sake of family izzat. Although *izzat* is still important, women are beginning to question a system that allows double standards in the behaviour and values for men and women and expects women to stay in marriages even where they are experiencing physical and mental abuse.

The drinking of alcohol is common within the Sikh community. Most Sikhs drink unless they are initiated or from particular sects. Most women under the age of forty in the survey admitted to drinking socially, although alcoholism is virtually non-existent. Sikh men are more prone to drinking alcohol to excess, which was one reason women gave for the break-up of their marriages. A few younger Sikh women smoke cigarettes, and taking drugs, although uncommon, is not unheard of. The Sikh community frowns upon both practices. Parents seem to have little understanding or awareness of drug addiction.

To conclude, Sikh women have adjusted well to life in the UK, whilst retaining a strong cultural and religious identity. This can create problems of dual identity for younger professional women in particular, and they are responding by breaking free from some of the more traditional practices which have consigned women to particular roles in the past. There is still a need for more support for women who do not fit readily into the expectations of their community and for increased tolerance and understanding of those who are striving to combine their personal development with the love they have for their community and culture.

Bibliography

Adi Granth. Amritsar: Shromani Gurdwara Prabandhak Committee (Standard version of 1430 pages in Punjabi).

Ahluwalia, M. M. *Kukas: The Freedom Fighters of Punjab.* New Delhi: Allied Publishers, 1965.

Bakshi, H. S. 'An approach to support services for the elderly'. In Sharma, M.L. and Dak, T. M (eds.). *Ageing in India: Challenge for the Society.* Delhi: Ajanta Publications, n.d.

Ballard, C. 'Arranged marriages in the British context'. *New Community,* 3, Summer, 1978, 181-196.

Ballard, C. 'Conflict, continuity and change: second generation South Asians'. In Khan, V.S. (ed.). *Minority Families in Britain: Support and Stress.* London: Macmillan, 1979.

Ballard, R. and Ballard C. 'The Sikhs: the development of South Asian settlements in Britain'. In Watson, J. L. (ed.). *Between Two Cultures.* Oxford: Basil Blackwell, 1977.

Ballard, R. 'The context and consequences of migration: Jullundhur and Mirpur compared'. In *New Community.* 11, 1983.

Ballard, R. 'Family organisation among the Sikhs in Britain'. In *New Community,* 2 , 1973, 12-23.

Basarke, A. *Where are the Women? Current Thoughts on Sikhism.* Chandigarh: Institute of Sikh Studies, 1996.

Basham, A. L. (ed.) *A Cultural History of India.* Oxford: Clarendon Press, 1975.

Bhachu, P. *Twice Migrants: East African Sikh Settlers in Britain.* London: Tavistock, 1985.

Brah, A. 'South Asian teenagers in Southall: their perceptions of marriage, family and ethnic identity'. In *New Community,* 6 (3),1978, 197-206.

Chadney, J.G. *The Sikhs of Vancouver.* New York: AMS Press, 1984.

Census. *Census 2001.* Office for National Statistics. April 2001.

Cole, W. O. 'Sikhism'. In *A Handbook of Living Religions* ed. by J. Hinnel. Harmondsworth: Penguin, 1984

Cole, W. O. and Sambhi, P.S. *The Sikhs: Their Religious Beliefs and Practices.* London: Routledge and Kegan Paul, 1978.

Crauford, Q. *Sketches of the Hindoos.* London: T. Cadell, 1790.

Desai, R. *Indian Immigrants in Britain.* London: Oxford University Press, 1963.

Dhanjal, B. 'Sikh women in Southall: some impressions'. In *New Community,* 5 (1-2), 1976, 109-114.

Drury, B. 'Sikh girls and the maintenance of an ethnic culture'. In *New Community,* 17 (3), 1991. 387-399.

Dube, S. C. *Indian Village*. London: Routledge and Kegan Paul, 1954.

Figes, E. *Patriarchal Attitudes*. London: Macmillan, 1970.

Ghai, D. P. *Portrait of a Minority Asians in East Africa*. Nairobi: Oxford University Press, 1965.

Ghuman, P. 'Bhatra Sikhs in Cardiff: family and kinship organisation'. In *New Community*, 8 (3), 1980. 308-316.

Ghurya, G. S. *Caste and Race in India*. Bombay: Popular Prakashan, 1969.

Helweg, A. W. *Sikhs in England: The Development of a Migrant Community*. Delhi: Oxford University Press, 1979.

Ibbetson, D, Mclagan, E. D. and Rose, H. A. *A Glossary of the Tribes and Castes of the Punjab and North-West Frontier Province. Vol. 1*, Lahore: 1919.

Ikram, A. *Pakistan and the Indian Heritage*. Lahore: Sang-e-meel, 1983.

James, A. G. *Sikh Children in Britain*. London: Oxford University Press, 1974.

Johar, S. S. *Handbook on Sikhism*. Delhi: Vivek Publishing Company, 1977.

Johnson, J. *The Path of the Masters*. Beas: Radha Soami Satsang, 1985.

Juergensmeyer, M and Barrier, N. G. (eds.) *Sikh Studies: Comparative Perspectives on a Changing Tradition*. Working papers from the Berkeley Conference on Sikh studies. Berkeley Religious Studies Series. Berkeley: Graduate Theological Union, 1979.

Jhutti, J. Dowry among Sikhs in Britain. In Menski, W. (ed.) *South Asians and the Dowry Problem*. Stoke on Trent: Trentham, 1998

Jyoti, S. K. *Marriage Practices of the Sikhs: A study of Inter-generational Differences*. Delhi: Deep and Deep, 1983.

Kalra, S. S. *Daughters of Tradition*. Birmingham: Diana Balbir Publications, 1980

Kalsi, S. S. *The Evolution of a Sikh Community in Britain*. Leeds: University of Leeds Community Religions Project, 1993.

Kapur, D. L. *Call of the Great Master*. Beas: Radha Soami Satsang, 1972.

Kaur, K. *Sikh Women: Fundamental Issues in Sikh Studies*. Chandigarh: Institute of Sikh Studies, 1992.

Kaur, U. *Sikh Religion and Economic Development*. New Delhi: National Book Organisation. 1990.

Kaur, Upinder Jit. *Sikh Religion and Economic Development*. New Delhi: National Book Organisation, 1990.

Kinsley, D. *Hindu Goddesses: Visions of the Divine Feminine in the Hindu Religious Tradition*. Berkeley: University of California Press, 1986.

Knott, K. *Hinduism in Leeds: A Study of Religious Practice in the Indian Hindu Community and Hindu-related Groups*. Leeds: University of Leeds Community Religions Project, 1986.

Kohli, S. S. *Sikh Ethics*. New Delhi: Manoharlal, 1975.

Macauliffe, M. R. *The Sikh Religion*. New York: Chand, 1963.

McLeod, W. H. *Sikhism: Textual Sources for the Study of Sikhism*, edited and translated by W. H. McLeod. Chicago: University of Chicago Press, 1990.

McMullen, C. O. *Religious Beliefs and Practices of the Sikhs in Rural Punjab*. London: Jaya Books, 1989.

Malcolm, J. (Sir). *Sketch of the Sikhs*. London: John Murray, 1812.

Mandelbaum, D. G. *Society in India: Continuity and Change*. Berkeley: University of California Press, 1972.

Manu, *The Laws of Manu*. In Buhler, G. (tr.) *Sacred Books of the East*, xxv, ed. by Max Muller. London: Oxford University Press, 1886.

Mayer, A. C. The significance of quasi-groups in the study of complex societies'. In Banton, M. (ed.). *The Social Anthropology of Complex Societies*. ASA monographs, London: Tavistock Publications, 1966.

Millett, K. *Sexual Politics*. London: Rupert Hart-Davis, 1969. Repr. 1971.

Morris, H. S. *Indians in Uganda*. London: Weidenfield and Nicholson, 1968.

Nirankari, M. S. 'Nirankaris'. *Bulletin of Christian Institute of Sikh Studies*. 7 (1), 1978. 2-10.

Oberoi, H. *The construction of Religious Boundaries: Culture, Identity and Diversity in the Sikh Traditions*. Delhi: Oxford University Press, 1994.

Peristiany, J.G. (ed.). *Honour and Shame: The Values of Mediterranean Society*. Chicago: The University of Chicago Press, 1966.

Radhakrishanan, S. *Religion and Society*. London: Allen and Unwin,1956.

Rose, E. J. B. *Colour and Citizenship*. London: Faber and Faber, 1969.

Sahlins, M. D. 'On the sociology of primitive exchange'. In Banton, M. (ed.). *The Relevance of Models for Social Anthropology. The Association for Social Anthropologists Monograph No. 2*. London: Tavistock Publications, 1965.

Scarman, Lord. *The Scarman Report. The Brixton Disorders 10-12 April 1981*. London: HMSO, 1981.

Shan, S. *In My Own Name: an Autobiography*. London: Women's Press, 1985.

Sharma, A. *Sati: Historical and Phenomenological Essay*. Delhi: Motilal Banarsidass, 1988.

Sharma, A. *Today's Woman in World Religions*. Albany: State University of New York Press, 1993.

Sharma, S. *Lok Gitan Vich Samajik Jiwan*. Amritsar: Ravi Sahit Prakashan, 1988.

Sikh Rahit Maryada. Amritsar: Shromani Gurdwara Prabandhak Committee, 1992.

Singh, A. *Ethics of the Sikhs*. Patiala: Punjab University,1991.

Singh, G. (tr.) *Guru Granth Sahib*. Amritsar: Shromani Gurdwara Prabandhak Committee, 1984.

Singh, G. *A History of the Sikh People (1469-1978)*. New Delhi: World Sikh University Press, 1979.

Singh, J. *The Sikh Revolution: A Perspective View*. New Delhi: Bahri, 1981.

Singh, K. *The Sikhs*. Calcutta: Lustre Press, 1984.

Singh, P. *The Sikhs*. London: John Murray, 1999

Singh, R. *The Sikh Community in Bradford*. Bradford: Bradford College, 1978.

Singh, T. *A Short History of the Sikhs. Vol. 1* (1469-1765). Patiala: Publication Bureau, 1969.

Singh, W. *Sikhism and Punjab's Heritage*. Patiala: Punjabi University,1990.

Tatla, D. S. *The Sikh Diaspora*. London: UCL Press, 1999.

Thomas, T. *The Way of the Guru*. Milton Keynes: Open University, 1978.

Welty, P. T. *The Asians: Their Heritage and Their Destiny. 3rd ed*. Philadelphia: J. B. Lippincot Company, 1963.

Wilson, A. *Finding a Voice: Asian Women in Britain*. London: Virago Press, 1978.

Young, K. K. Women in Hinduism. In Sharma, A. *Today's Woman in World Religion*. Albany: State University of New York Press, 1993.

Punjabi Literature

Adi Granth. Amritsar: Shromani Gurdwara Prabandhak Committee. (Standard version of 1430 pages in Punjabi)

Sharma, S. *Lok Gitan Vich Samajik Jiwan*. Amritsar: Ravi Sahit Prakashan, 1988.

Sikh Rahit Maryada. Amritsar: Sharomani Gurdwara Prabandhak Committee, 1992.

Periodicals and documents to which reference has been made:
Des Prades, London; *New Community*, London; *Satjug Weekly*, New Delhi

Glossary

Ab	Water
Adi Granth Sahib	Early edition of Granth, a sacred Sikh scripture
Akal Purakh	God, not affected by death or time
Akal Takht	Supreme authority
Akhandpath	Continuous reading of the *Guru Granth Sahib*, taking 48 hours
Amrit	Nectar, a solution of water and sugar used at Sikh ceremonies
Amrit-chhakna	To undergo initiation ceremony
Amritdhari	An initiated Sikh
Amrit Pahul	A Sikh initiation ceremony
Amrit Prachar	A Sikh initiation ceremony
Anand Karaj	Sikh marriage ceremony
Anandpur Sahib	Holy city of Sikhs
Ardas	Sikh prayer recited at the conclusion of a service
Arora	A trading caste
Baba	a) A term used for paternal grandfather b) A term used for respected and religious men
Baisakhi/Vaisakhi	a) New year for Sikhs b) An important Sikh festival celebrated to mark the birth of the *Khalsa*
Bani	Speech – a term collectively used for the compositions of the *Gurus* and the saints included in the *Guru Granth Sahib*
Baradari	See *Biradari*

Barat	The groom's marriage party
Barh	A tree, Bengalensis
Barkat	Prosperity
Basant Panchami	Festival marking the beginning of Spring
Beas	The name of a river
Bhadan	Hindu ceremony of cutting hair for the first time
Bhai	a) Brother b) A term used to describe outstanding men c) A term used for the custodian of a *gurdwara.*
Bhana manana	Accepting the will of God
Bhangra	Punjabi folk dance
Bharjayi	A term used for sister-in-law
Bhatra	A Sikh caste group: *granthis* and fortune-tellers
Bhawan	*Nirankari* place of worship
Bhindi	Okra, an Indian vegetable
Bhog	Finishing ceremony of the reciting of *Guru Granth Sahib*
Bhua	Father's sister
Bhut	Male evil spirit or a ghost
Bhutni	Female evil spirit
Biradari	Refers both to brotherhood and caste group; the term is used by Sikhs, Muslims and Punjabi Hindus
Boliyan	Folk songs and tales
Brahm	Another name for God
Brahman	Priestly caste of Hindus
Burkah	A kind of veil, covering from face to toe
Chacha	Father's younger brother
Chachi	Wife of father's younger brother
Chadar	Shawl-like veil to cover body
Chadar pauna	Widow's remarriage ceremony
Chakri	A sharp edged steel discus
Chamar	A caste name, leather worker
Chapati/chappati	Flat bread
Charanamat	*Amrit* from washing the feet

Charpai	An Indian cot
Chauri	Ritual fan made of yak hair waved over the *Guru Granth Sahib*: symbol of authority
Chenab	The name of a river
Chunni	A headscarf
Chura	A set of red bangles given to the bride by her mother's brother before the wedding at the *chaura* ceremony
Churel	A female ghost
Daaj	Dowry
Daan	Charitable gifts for which no return is expected
Dal	Pulses
Darani	Wife of husband's younger brother
Darbar Sahib	A term used for the Golden Temple
Darri	Cotton carpet
Darshan	Pilgrimage or seeing the divine
Daswandh	Donating one tenth of one's earning for religious purposes
Daya	Kindness
Deevas	Earthen lamp
Dera	Headquarters
Devnagri/Devanagri	Hindi script
Devi	Deity
Devi mata	Goddess – also used for a pious woman
Devta	Deity, Demi-god
Dhaga taveet	Amulet
Dharam	a) Social and religious obligations b) A Punjabi term used for religion
Dharti-mata	Mother Earth
Dhole	A large two-sided drum
Dholki	A wooden drum
Diwali	Festival of lights celebrated by Hindus and Sikhs normally in October or November
Diwan	A term used for Sikh act of worship i.e. Sunday *diwan*
Doaba	The plain tract of central Punjab bounded by the Beas and Sutlej rivers

Doli	Departure of the wedding party
Dupatta	Headscarf
Ek jyot duo murti	One spirit in two bodies
Gatka	Martial arts
Geet	Folk songs
Ghagra	Heavy pleated long skirt
Ghee	Clarified butter
Ghiya	Courgettes
Ghund	Veil covering face
Giddha	Folk dance mainly performed by women
Goan	Music sessions on happy occasions
Gora	A term used for white man
Gori	Term used for white female
Got /Gotra	Surnames
Gou-mata	Mother cow
Granth	Book, literary composition
Granth Sahib	See *Guru Granth Sahib*
Granthi	One who looks after the *Granth Sahib* – a reader of the *Granth Sahib* – may also be a custodian of *gurdwara*
Gugga Puja	Snake worship
Gurbani	Religious hymns
Gurdwara	Literally the house of the *Guru* – a Sikh temple
Gurmantar	*Guru*'s words
Gur-maryada	According to Sikh religion
Gurmat	*Guru*'s teachings
Gurmukhi	Script used for writing Punjabi
Guru	Religious teacher or a preceptor
Guru Granth Sahib	The Sikh Holy scripture
Guru-Maryada	Compulsory rituals in the presence of the *Guru Granth Sahib*
Gurupurb	Anniversary of the birth or death of Sikh *Gurus*
Gutka	Collection of Hymns
Haja	See *haya*
Halal	Slaughtered by the process of a gradual killing
Hankar	Pride

Haumen	Individualism or self-centredness
Havan	Fire worship – popular among *Namdhari* Sikhs
Havankund	Fire altar
Haya	Modesty
Hazur Sahib	A Sikh holy place
Hola Mohalla	A Sikh festival when mock battles are held between *Nihang* warriors at Anandpur Sahib
Holi	A Hindu festival held at the full moon in February-March
Ik Onkar	One God – used as a Sikh emblem
Izzat	Family honour
Jaidad	Family wealth
Jajmani	Patron-client relationship
Janam Sakhis	Life stories of Sikh *Gurus*
Jat	Land-owning class
Jathani	Wife of husband's elder brother
Jathera	A place for ancestor worship
Jat Pat	Caste system
Jatha	Organisation
Jehad	Crusade, holy war
Jhara	Touching of afflicted part by a wise man
Jhatka	Mode of beheading an animal with one stroke
Jheer/Jhir	Male person belonging to the Water-carrier caste
Jhelum	The name of a river
Jhutha	a) Eating or tasting food with the same spoon and giving it to someone else b) A liar
Julaha	Male person belonging to weaver caste
Kacch	Loose fitting underwear – one of the five *K*s
Kam	Lust
Kameez	Tunic or long shirt
Kanga/Kangha	Comb – one of the five *K*s
Kara	Bangle – one of the five *K*s

Karah prasad	Mixture of semolina, sugar and butter – blessed food shared at the end of Sikh services
Karmai	Engagement
Kartik/Katak	A lunar month that falls in October-November
Karva chauth	Fast kept for the long life of husband
Katha	Story
Kathakar	Story-teller
Kaur	Name assumed by all female Sikhs – literally 'princess'
Keertan/kirtan	Hymn singing
Kes/Kesh	Uncut hair – one of the five *K*s
Keshadhari	One who wears his/her hair long or uncut
Khadar	Coarse cotton
Khalsa	a) The Sikh order, brotherhood instituted by the tenth *Guru* in 1699. b) The Pure Ones
Khalsa Panth	Sikh religious order
Khanda	Double-edged sword – one of the emblems of Sikhism
Khandan	Family standing/dynasty
Khande da amrit	See *Khande di pahul*
Khande di pahul	Initiation ceremony
Khatri	a) A mercantile caste b) A male person belonging to *Khatri* caste
Khes	A woven figured fabric
Khidmat	Hospitality
Kirpan	Sword – one of the five *K*s
Kirt karo	Earning living by honest and approved means
Kirtan	Hymn singing
Kismet	Luck
Kowli	Soup plate
Krodh	Anger
Kuk	Shriek
Kuka	A word used for a *Namdhari* Sikh
Kurmai	Engagement

Laaj	Shyness/modesty/honour
Ladoos	Indian sweet distributed on auspicious occasions
Langar	Free food served to all in *gurdwaras*
Lashkara	A Punjabi TV channel
Lattha	Stiff cotton
Lavan	Hymns read out from the *Guru Granth Sahib* at the wedding ceremony
lavan	Walking around the *Guru Granth Sahib* during the marriage ceremony
Lehgha choli	Long pleated skirt and short blouse
Len den	Gifts given to in-laws
Lobh	Greed
Lohri	Harvest festival
Lokgeet	Folk-songs
Maghi	Harvest festival
Maiyan	A pre-wedding ceremony – the bride and groom are rubbed with a paste of flour, mustard oil and turmeric
Majha	Region in the Punjab
Malwa	Region in the Punjab
Mama	Mother's brother
Mami	Wife of mother's brother
Marhi masan	Graves and graveyards
Masad/Masar	Husband of mother's sister
Masi	Mother's sister
Matha Tekna	Bow down out of respect
Maya	Money, wealth, illusion
Mehendi/Mehdi	Henna used in marriage ceremonies by Indian women to decorate hands and feet
Mela	Fair/festival
Milni	Ritual meeting of the family members of both sides before the wedding ceremony
Miri and *Piri*	Temporal and spiritual
Moh	Worldly attachment and obsessions
Mool Mantar	Important part of *Japji*, religious hymns
Mooth	A kind of pulse
Muhabbat	Affection or love

Muklava	Post-wedding ceremony before the consummation of marriage
Mukti	Liberation
Mundan	First hair cutting ceremony
Murti-puja	Idol or Image worship
Murva dola	Return visit by bride with her in-laws' family
Nai	Barber, member of low caste
Nam	God's name
Nam Japna	The reciting of God's name
Nam Laina	Taking and receiving God's name
Namaz	Prayers offered by the Muslims
Namdharis	A Sikh movement: followers of *Baba* Ram Singh – *Namdharis* believe in a living *guru*
Namsimran	Meditation on God's name
Nana	Mother's father
Nanan	Husband's sister
Nani	Mother's mother
Nankana Sahib	Birth Place of *Guru* Nanak in Talwandi (Pakistan)
Natth	Nose jewellery
Nihang	A Sikh sect – its members wear traditional uniform of Sikh soldiers
Nimarta	Humility
Nirankar	Without form – used for God
Nirankari	A religious sect
Nishan Sahib	Sikh flag
Pali	Language of Buddhist scriptures
Palla frowna	Giving-away ceremony
Panchayat	Council of elders
Pangat	Sitting in a row without caste and class distinction
Panj	Five
Panj pyare	Five beloved Sikhs
Panth	A term used for Sikh order
Paranthas	A fried or stuffed *chapati*
Patasha	Sugar crystal
Path-bhog	Finishing ceremony of the recitation of the *Granth Sahib*

Phulkari	Hand embroidery of Punjab
Phuphar	Husband of father's sister
Pipal	A tree called Ficus religiosa
Pir	Muslim saints
Pirhi	Generation
Pitr	Ancestor
Pitr-puja	Ancestor worship
Pitt siapa	Women hit different parts of their bodies with their hands when someone dies
Prasad	Mixture of sugar, semolina and butter
Pret	Free roaming of spirit
Pret-ruh	Roaming spirit
Punjabi	a) The language of Punjab b) People of Punjab
Purdah	Veil
Puris	A thin type of fried bread
Qur'an	Holy book of Muslims
Radhasoami	A religious sect
Ragi	Hymn-singers
Rahit Maryada	Sikh code of conduct
Rahit Nama	Document on the Sikh code of conduct
Raj	Empire
Ramgarhia	A Sikh artisan caste comprising carpenters, blacksmiths, masons, or village artisans
Rashbhari	Raspberry
Ravidasi	Untouchables
Robh	Influence
Robhdar	An influential person
Rockna	Reservation of prospective groom by the bride's family.
Romalla/Rumallas	Expensive cloth to cover the *Guru Granth Sahib*
Saag	A kind of cooked mixed vegetable puree mainly from green mustard
Sabzi	Vegetable
Sadharan/sehaj path	A non-continuous reading of the *Granth Sahib*
Sagan	Auspicious gift or act

Sahejdhari	Sikh who believes in the teachings of Sikhism but not in Sikh identity
Sainchi	*Guru Granth Sahib* in two volumes
Saledi	Evil spirit, who can take human form without casting shadow
Salwar	Loose trousers worn by Punjabi and Muslim women
Samadhi	Tombs associated with Hindu and Sikh saints
Samagam	Celebration
Sampat Path	Recitation by repeating *gurbani*
Sampuran	Complete
Sangat	Congregation
Sangrand	First day of the lunar month
Sant	A pious man
Santmat	Principles and traditions set up by saints
Santokh	Contentment
Sanyas/Sanyasa	Renunciation
Sarafat	Nobleness
Saree/sari	Female dress, made from six metres of fabric
Satguru	A true teacher
Sati	The burning of widows on their husband's funeral pyre
Satsang	Weekly *kirtan* sessions
Seva	Voluntary service to the community
Shabad	Hymns
Shahan Shah	King of Kings
Sharadh/Shradh	Food given to Brahmans for the dead
Sharam	Modesty
Sharika	Element of jealousy among *Biradari* members
Shaunk	Stir-fry
Shingar	Ornament
Shishya	Disciple
Shiv ji da vart	Fasting for the blessing of Lord Shiva – a Hindu god
Shromani Gurdwara Prabandhak Committee	An authoritative Sikh religious committee based in Amritsar, Punjab
Siana	Wise man or a healer

Sidhi-turban	*Namdhari* turban style
Sikhya	Teachings, advice
Sindhi	Language of Sindh, embroidery
Singh	Literally 'lion' – the name assumed by male members of the *Khalsa panth*
Sodhi	*Namdhari* initiated Sikh
Sonnera	Pedestal
Souff	Cotton satin
Suhag	a) Marriage songs b) Husband
Suraj-Devta	Sun God
Sutak	Contamination at the birth of a child
Tarka	Fried onion mixture added to *dal*
Taya	Father's elder brother
Tayi	Wife of father's elder brother
Tera bhana mitha lagay	Accepting God's will
Thakka	A ceremony to reserve a prospective bridegroom
Thal	A plate of metal
Tikka	a) Gold jewellery for forehead b) Mark made on the forehead with a sandal paste or vermillion
Tilwar	Sword
Toka taki	Criticism, fault finding
Tola	Gold measurement
Tulsi	Indian basil
Ujha	Sorcerer
Vaidaygi	Departure of bride
Vak	Opening sentence from the *Guru Granth Sahib*
Vanprastha	Renunciation
Varsi	Anniversary
Vata satha	Exchange
Vayen	Lamenting by recounting the virtues of a deceased person
Viah	The wedding ceremony
Viakhia	Explaining the religious traditions
Waheguru/Vaheguru	To praise the Lord by saying 'Wonderful Lord'
Wand chhako	Share with the less fortunate
Zamindari	Land ownership

Index

Ablution 66
Adi Granth 19, 21, 22, 25, 26, 33, 35, 41, 48, 49, 50, 51, 62, 63, 66, 77
Africanisation 7, 8
Akhand-Path 13, 27, 42, 43, 122
Alcoholism 167
Amritdhari 13
Amritsar 18
Anand Karaj 33
Arabic 3
Aroras 96
Arranged marriages 95, 96, 97, 98, 99, 100101, 102, 105, 106, 107, 108, 133, 139, 146, 162, 163
Asceticism 49

Baba Puran Singh 5, 42, 13
Baba Vishvakarma 21, 40
Basant Panchami 42, 43
Beas 2
Bhai gurdas 19
Bhangra 78, 80, 81
Bhatras 7, 9, 63, 64, 110
Bhog 42
Birth(s) 32, 71, 72, 116, 122, 132, 143
Black magic 22, 164
Brahman (s) 18

Caste(s) 4, 7, 8, 10, 11, 18, 25, 26, 29, 32, 40, 49, 55, 59, 96, 97, 98 99, 100, 101, 105, 107, 163, 164

Caste system 8, 11, 25, 100, 101, 162, 164
Celibacy 22
Chamars 7, 9
Chapatis 62, 66, 80
Charity 66
Charpais 120
Chenab 2
Churels 124
Class system 164
Classical music 82
Code of conduct 17, 20, 43
Communal 37
Congregation 24, 33, 35, 36, 38, 49
Cremation 35, 77
Culture 95
Customs 14

Daswandh 13, 24
Deities 121
Devanagri 3
Devotinal music 81
Direct Migrants 7
Discrimination 86, 87, 136, 157
Divorce 105, 107, 129, 139, 141, 150, 152, 166, 167
Diwali 43, 78, 79, 80, 82, 92, 124, 151
Diwan 10, 11, 13, 28, 37, 43, 44
Doaba(ians) 3, 5, 7, 97, 153
Dowry 50, 52, 58, 73, 76, 95, 108, 110, 111, 112, 132, 134, 135 141, 163

Drinking 91, 167
Drug-taking 92, 167

East Africa 4, 5, 6, 7, 13, 55, 56, 72, 97, 98, 125, 127, 130
East African migrants 8
East African Sikhs 98, 159
East Punjab 2
Endogamous marriages 98
Equality 18, 24, 25, 26, 27, 40, 47, 51, 54, 72, 157, 164
Evil sprits 45, 119, 123
Exorcist 124
Extended family 95, 147, 148, 161, 163

Family prestige 128
Fanaticism 17
Fast(ing) 66, 164
Female foetuses 52
Five takhts 41
Folk beliefs 125
Folk dancing 80
Folk music 80, 82
Folk songs 67, 81, 82
Folk tradition(s) 95, 118, 119
Forced marriages 95
Forced migration 7
Funeral 77

Gender equality 26, 47, 51, 72
Generosity 67
Genetic diseases 96
Giddha 80, 81

Golden Temple 18, 41
Gori 102
Gotra(s) 25, 96, 97, 98,
    100, 101, 107
Granth Sahib 18, 19, 122
Granthis 7, 27, 32, 35, 37,
    42, 49, 73, 125
Gurbani 19, 23, 34, 37, 73,
    153
Gurdwara(s) 3, 4, 5, 10, 12,
    13, 17, 19, 20, 21, 22,
    23, 24, 25, 26, 27, 32
    33, 34, 35, 36, 37, 38,
    39, 40, 41, 42, 43, 44,
    45, 51, 64, 67, 69, 71,
    73, 74, 75, 76, 80, 85,
    90, 103, 104, 118, 125,
    137, 163, 164
Gurmat 17
Gurmukhi 3, 18, 21, 37
Guru Amardas 25, 49, 51
Guru Angad 18
Guru Arjun 18, 19, 26, 36,
    42
Guru Gobind Singh 9, 12,
    17, 18, 20, 22, 25, 29,
    30, 31, 42, 49
Guru Granth Sahib 9, 10,
    12, 17, 18, 19, 20, 21,
    27, 32, 33, 34, 35, 36,
    37, 38, 39, 40, 42, 43,
    47, 48, 51, 73, 104
Guru Hargobind 18, 43, 50
Guru Nanak 9, 17, 18, 22,
    24, 29, 35, 42, 47, 48,
    49, 82
Guru Tegh Bahadur 42
Gurumantar 13
Gurupurbs 37, 39, 42
Gutka 19

Haja 14
Halal 63
Haryana 3
Haumen 10
Havan 34
Hindu(s) 18, 47, 62, 66,
    164
Hinduism 18, 47
Hola 42, 43, 44
Holi 79
Holika 79
Hospitality 66, 67

Hypogamous marriages 96
Identity 5, 8, 9, 18, 29, 30,
    39, 102, 148, 159, 160,
    163, 167
Ik Onkar 20, 21
Image worship 22
Immolation 50
Infanticide 26.47, 48, 50,
    52
Initiation 10, 17, 21, 29,
    30, 43, 49, 160
Institutional racism 136
Inter-caste marriges 100,
    107
Islam 18, 47, 51
Isolation 86, 89, 90, 91,
    118, 138, 166
Izzat 14, 53, 58, 85, 90,
    104, 106, 110, 128,
    132, 133, 148, 161, 167

Jajmani system 8
Janam Sakhi 19, 20
Jat 7, 8, 9, 96, 100
Jatha 13
Jatheras 121, 122, 164
Jhatka 63
Jhelum 2
Jhirs 7, 9, 100
Joint family(ies) 112, 113,
    114, 115, 116, 117, 130
Joint living 112, 113, 114,
    129, 161
Julahas 7, 9

Khalsa Panth 25, 30, 43, 78
Khalsa 9, 18, 25, 29
Khanda 21
Khatris 7
Khatris 8, 9, 96
Khidmat 14
Kirt Karo 23, 28
Kirtan 37, 43, 44, 82, 90,
    92, 104, 164, 166

Laaj 14
Laaj 53
Langar 10, 11, 12, 18, 23,
    24, 25, 27, 36, 37, 43,
    44, 49, 64, 71, 164
Lavan 33, 34, 75
Lifestyle 61, 62, 71, 92, 99,
    102, 159, 161

Living standards 6, 61, 62,
    141
Lohri 43, 44, 79, 80
Love marriages 102, 162

Maghi 44
Magical Healing 95, 123
Majha 97
Malwa(i) 97
Marriage(s) 32, 33, 72, 73,
    74, 75, 76, 95, 96, 97,
    98, 99, 100, 101, 102,
    105, 106, 107, 110,
    111, 116, 117, 119,
    133, 134, 137, 139,
    141, 146, 147, 150,
    151, 155, 157, 160,
    162, 163, 166, 167
Marriage practices 96
Marriage rituals 73
Marriage tradition 98
Matrilineal relations 116,
    128
Migration 6, 7
Mixed marriages 99, 102,
    103, 104, 105, 108, 166
Mono-culture 136
Monogamy 50
Muhabbat 14
Murtipuja 21

Nais 7, 9
Namdharis 9, 12, 24, 33,
    34, 38, 42, 43, 63, 76
Naming 160
Namsimran 12, 34, 20, 21
Nani 149
Nature worship 123
Nirankaris 9, 11, 21, 64
Nishan sahib 21
Nishkam Sevak Jatha 9, 42,
    63

Pangat 23, 24, 49
Partition 6
Patriarchal 47, 53
Patrilineage 116, 160
Pilgrimage 41
Polygamy 47, 52
Punjab 1, 2, 5, 6, 8
Punjabi 1, 2, 3, 18, 38, 153,
    159, 164